One Half the People:
The Fight for Woman Suffrage

Anne F. Scott

Duke University

Andrew M. Scott

University of North Carolina

The America's Alternatives Series
Edited by Harold M. Hyman

One Half the People:
The Fight for Woman Suffrage

J. B. Lippincott Company
Philadelphia/New York/Toronto

ISBN 0-397-47333-8
Library of Congress Catalog Card Number 74-28032
Printed in the United States of America

1 3 5 7 9 8 6 4 2

Library of Congress Cataloging in Publication Data

Scott, Anne Firor
    One half the people.

    (The America's alternatives series)
    Bibliography: p.
    1. Women—Suffrage—United States. I. Scott,
Andrew MacKay, joint author. II. Title.
JK1896.S36   324'.3'0973   74-28032
ISBN 0-397-47333-8

Contents

Foreword

Each volume in the "America's Alternatives" series seeks to explain why decision-makers in crucial historical choice situations adopted one course and rejected others. The author may ask about the information or assumptions on which decisions were based, prevalent public attitudes or other operative constraints, and about the impact of a given decision on the future course of American history. This volume asks such questions but with certain differences from other titles in the series.

A series designed to deal with fundamental alternatives in the American past could not ignore the long-drawn out struggle to enfranchise women. The story covers more than a hundred years and as the Professors Scott note, suffrage "became the symbolic focus of feminism, and as a result the woman movement for a while took on the semblance of a single issue movement." As the authors examined their material it became clear that what they were seeing was a slow process of education and the encouragement of attitudinal change throughout a whole society. In this small documents-supported volume, they reevaluate the dynamics of this protracted conflict between two incompatible sets of ideals, both of which were attractive to Americans and well-grounded in American traditions. These ideals were, on the one hand, the democratic ideology with its emphasis on equality and self-government and, on the other, established social views concerning the proper role of women.

The ongoing debate was conducted in homes and on street corners and in state and national legislatures. A nation whose electorate was almost exclusively male, marched at a slow cadence while it considered the desirability of enfranchising females. It was inherent in the nature of this sluggish process, the Scotts realized, that no single leader such as a president or group of decision makers held the balance of power in the palm of a hand. Therefore, almost until the last stages of the battle for the woman suffrage amendment to the Constitution, no single alternative point became visible.

This fact created some differences between this volume and others in the series, though it remains in fundamental harmony with the series' concept and major physical arrangements. Like the other titles in the series, Part One of this volume is a narrative and analytical historical essay. But unlike the others, the Scotts' engaging volume on female enfranchisement reaches no Alternative decisional public policy crossroad until very late in Part One. Again, like other titles in the series, the Scott volume contains in whole or in part, many appropriate source documents that illustrate Part One. Unlike the others, the Part Two Documents in the Scott's volume are not, by definition, keyed to Part One Alternatives until the final one. As in the other titles, this volume's Part Three offers further guidance in form of a bibliographic essay.

By now suffrage, long the single focus of many women's rights trailblazers, has been with us for more than half a century. Sensitivity to the multiple obstacles to women's realization of social and individual goals has increased. The Scotts show why women wanted to vote and how they overcame the cultural forces which had long denied them the right to do so, and by implication throw considerable light on feminism in our own time.

Harold M. Hyman
Rice University

Preface

Why have we written a book about the woman suffrage movement?

Because that movement was important and has been neglected in the study of American history and of American politics. The suffrage movement was a major social movement, which at its peak absorbed the energies of hundreds of thousands and represented a vital extension of the democratic principle. Although it has had a powerful influence on the position of women in American life, it is usually passed over silently in traditional history texts. Political scientists, who devote considerable attention to other constitutional amendments, sometimes have trouble remembering what the Nineteenth Amendment was, and introductory texts in political science mention it only in passing.

Until quite recently most historians and political scientists have been men, and have tended to view things relating to women as not really very important. This is beginning to change, and some of the developments in the American past in which women played a major part or which were important for women are being studied and written about.

The woman suffrage movement is likely to be of particular interest to contemporary women in search of liberation. The detailed issues and circumstances have changed, but the cultural conservatism and male prejudice which postponed the vote for women until 1920 remain. An analysis of the dynamics of the earlier movement—its progress, its problems—is therefore illuminating in the light of present concerns.

Millions of words have been written about woman suffrage but most of them are polemical or purely descriptive of events. In these essays the authors, a woman historian and a male political scientist, have sought to interpret and analyze. We have asked ourselves such questions as:

1. Who were the women who took the lead in asking for suffrage and what enabled them to be effective?

2. How did the strategy and tactics of the suffrage movement change and adapt over the years? What tactics and methods brought success in the end?
3. Why did the suffrage movement split, twice, and what were the consequences of these splits?
4. Why were so many men so strongly opposed to woman suffrage?
5. How did the suffrage movement fit into "progressivism" after 1900?
6. How did the Woman's Christian Temperance Union and the host of voluntary organizations contribute to the movement?

We found that a computer analysis of roll call votes in the two houses of Congress sharpened our perceptions of some of the changes taking place during the last five years before the amendment was ratified.

In selecting documents we have sought to cover the full range of thinking on the subject of woman suffrage while letting the participants speak for themselves. The documents say a good deal about the people who made up the movement, their concerns, and the methods they used.

Many of the participants in the suffrage movement were conscious of the historic significance of what they were doing. Succeeding scholars are in debt to Elizabeth Cady Stanton, Susan B. Anthony, Matilda Joselyn Gage and, later, Ida Husted Harper, for collecting and publishing the raw materials of part of the suffrage movement. These women represented one wing of the movement during the split which lasted from 1869 to 1890. The other wing has not yet found its historian, although much of the material for its history is to be found in the *Woman's Journal*, published from 1870 under the capable editorship of various members of the Blackwell family. Carrie Chapman Catt also made strenuous efforts to preserve the historical record. Her book and those of Maud Wood Park and Inez Haynes Irwin are the principal firsthand accounts of the later stages of the suffrage movement.

Anne Firor Scott
Duke University

Andrew MacKay Scott
University of North Carolina

Acknowledgments ⸻

We owe a special debt to Ellen DuBois who shared with us a great deal of unpublished material on the period 1848-1870, and who made a major contribution to our understanding of what was happening in the movement during those years. Professor DuBois, Dr. Louise M. Young, Rebecca Scott, Peter Railton and Harold Hyman all read the entire manuscript and made many helpful suggestions. Dara DeHaven, Paula Schwartz, Virginia Williams and Thomas Sloan have been the best kind of research assistants: those with minds of their own. With the usual absolution from blame for any sins properly ours, we thank them all.

Part One

One Half
the People

1

Consent of the Governed

> We hold these truths to be self-evident: that all men and women are created equal; that they are endowed by their Creator with certain inalienable rights . . .
>
> Declaration of Sentiments, 1848

The Early Beginnings

To late twentieth-century minds, sensitized by the most recent concern with feminism, the great political debates of the late eighteenth century have a strange ring. In all the weighty discussions leading up to the American Revolution and the making of the federal Constitution, it was taken for granted that the doctrine of natural rights and consent of the governed applied only to men. Thinkers and orators declaiming the Rights of Man meant the rights of men; the major theorists of libertarian thought ignored women. Along with slaves and indentured servants, for the purposes of law and politics women were simply not persons. Few people seemed to think it curious that one half the population should be thus ruled out of the process of self-government.

To be sure Mistress Margaret Brent, in 1647, had boldly asked the Maryland Assembly to grant her *two* votes, one in her own capacity as a freeholder, and one because she was the executor of Leonard Calvert, the recently deceased governor. According to the Archives of Maryland the governor "denyed that the sd Mrs. Brent should have any vote in the house," to which the said Mrs. Brent retorted that she would in that case protest all the proceedings of the assembly unless she might be present and vote.[1] Doubtless if the governor had been asked to justify his peremptory denial of her request he would have offered some homily about the proper role of females. Thus it would be for a long time: men in power confronted with the notion that women could be citizens with natural rights countered with confident assertions about their natural frailty, God's intentions with respect to woman's place in the scheme of things, and with the fact that in the common law husband and wife were one, and that one the husband (Document 1). Since voting was closely tied to owning property and married women could not own property, that took care of that.

By 1776, Americans were well along the way to accepting the doctrine of natural rights and the principle that just government rested on the consent of the governed, but neither was interpreted as giving political rights to women. Yet the logic of these principles pointed to a widening of the suffrage, and, in fact, in the next half-century nearly all white men would be enfranchised. For

3

women the logic of democracy worked more slowly. The equality of men went hand in hand with the inferiority of women. Men had a right to say how they were governed; women needed to be ruled by men for their own good. In short, the political ideals of the society pointed one way, the cultural assumptions another. The sustained tension between natural rights doctrines and assumptions about the nature of woman provided the basic dynamic for a struggle which would last for over a hundred years.

The long delay in enfranchising women was the result of the depth of male conviction about women's "true nature," and of male fear of anything which threatened to change the established pattern of relations between the sexes. Any analysis of the struggle for woman's suffrage must go beyond politics to deeply held cultural beliefs. Anthropologists have long understood that the definition of the male and female roles is central to the structure of a culture, and that anything which seems to threaten those definitions is bound to arouse strong feelings and powerful resistance. Horace Greeley was only more open than most opponents of woman suffrage when he told a correspondent in 1867: "It seems but fair to add that female suffrage seems to me to involve the balance of the family relation as it has hitherto existed . . ."[2]

Historians are becoming aware that the long struggle for woman suffrage can only be understood as part of the larger "woman question" which was one of the basic social conflicts of the nineteenth century. The history of the suffrage movement is, in part, the history of efforts to alter deeply rooted patterns of socialization. Unless we understand the pervasive male fear and prejudice, the length of the struggle becomes inexplicable. No effort will be made here to analyze the sources or origins of this prejudice. It will be taken as given, for its roots are lost in time and it exists in many different cultures.

After 1647 the question of women voting did not surface again for over a century. A few weeks before the adoption of the Declaration of Independence, John Adams received a letter from a constituent who wanted to broaden the suffrage in Massachusetts by reducing the property qualification for voters. Adams replied that, certainly, the only moral foundation upon which a government could rest was consent of the people.

> But to what extent shall we carry this principle? Shall we say that every individual of the community, old and young, male and female, as well as rich and poor, must consent, expressly, to every act of legislation? No, you will say, this is impossible. How, then, does the right arise in the majority to govern the minority against their will? Whence arises the right of the men to govern the women, without their consent?[3]

Answering his own question Adams followed Blackstone (who, in turn, had relied on Montesquieu), and argued that the purpose of property qualifications was to exclude people who were dependent on others to feed, clothe and employ them, and whose vote could thus be controlled. Widening the suffrage, Adams thought, would have dangerous and unforeseen consequences. If men who had no property should be permitted to vote, there would be no reason to forbid women the franchise, "for, generally speaking, women and children have as good judgements, and as independent minds, as those men who are wholly destitute of property." He advised his correspondent to avoid opening the subject and giving rise to "so fruitful a source of controversy ... New claims will arise; women will demand the vote."[3]

Perhaps Adams's sensitivity to the possibility of women demanding the vote was related to a letter he had recently received from his wife, in which she had argued forcefully that if there was to be a new Code of Laws it should recognize the rights of women. "Do not put such unlimited power into the hands of Husbands," she had written; all men had the potential for being tyrants, and women would not hold themselves bound "by any laws in which we have no voice, or Representation" (Document 2). She had learned her political theory well. Adams had replied lightly, but not without prescience:

> As to your extraordinary Code of Laws, I cannot but laugh. We have been told that our Struggle has loosened the bonds of Government everywhere. That Children and Apprentices were disobedient—that Schools and Colleges were grown turbulent—that Indians slighted their Guardians and Negroes grew insolent to their Masters. But your Letter was the first Intimation that another Tribe more numerous and powerful than all the rest were grown discontented. ..."[4]

If a man married to so extraordinary a woman as Abigail Adams could not take seriously the demands of women for self-government then the road ahead was destined to be long. John Adams made his little joke, but Abigail didn't laugh. She expressed her disappointment in a letter to her friend Mercy Otis Warren. She and Mrs. Warren had listened to many discussions of natural rights, and no one had ever been able to explain to them why the doctrine of consent should apply to men only.[5]

Stirring political discussions of liberty and the rights of men could not fail to stimulate some women to examine their own condition. In 1779 a contemporary of Abigail Adams wrote "On the Equality of the Sexes" in which she argued that "our souls are by nature *equal* to yours ... " and blamed the lesser accomplishments of women upon their inferior education.[6]

Another offshoot of the late eighteenth-century revolutionary ferment was Mary Wollstonecraft's *Vindication of the Rights of Women*, which appeared in England in 1792 and quickly made its way across the Atlantic. A Philadelphia Quaker reflected the atmosphere among the avant-garde in her city when she wrote, in the privacy of her journal, that Wollstonecraft "in many of her sentiments speaks my mind."[7] A year or so earlier a young woman had spoken before the Young Ladies' Academy of Philadelphia deploring women's political disabilities, and Charles Brockden Brown, another Philadelphian, in 1793 published a feminist novel, *Alcuin*.

Anne Bingham, replying to a letter from Thomas Jefferson in which he spoke slightingly of the frivolity of French ladies, disagreed with him, remarking that French women had political influence American women should envy.[8]

Such small straws in the wind could be multiplied, but the only practical change in women's political status was the curious case of their brief enfranchisement in New Jersey where, from 1790 to 1807, women were permitted to and did vote. How this came about is not at all clear, except that in drawing up a state constitution the convention of 1776 had provided that "all inhabitants" having certain qualifications might vote. A general election law of 1783 repeated the provision, and a subsequent election law spoke of voters as "he or she," indicating that "all inhabitants" did indeed mean women as well as men. In at least one election in the 1790s women were particularly active. There was spirited discussion of women voters in the newspapers, and after a corrupt and contested election in 1807 the legislature again amended the election laws. Declaring it "highly necessary to the safety, quiet, good order and dignity of the state," they proceeded to deprive women of the right to vote. The new law specified that electors were to be free white men. Thus the brief history of women voters in New Jersey ended, and as far as a close student of the matter could discover, there was no protest on the part of women themselves.[9]

The Growth of an Idea

Gradually, as the nineteenth century got underway, revolutionary enthusiasm, gave way to other concerns, and for a number of reasons a more conservative view of women's role developed. Nevertheless the idea that women might have a part to play in governing the society did not disappear completely. In 1820 in a Massachusetts constitutional convention, some members suggested that unmarried women who owned property ought to be enfranchised. In 1836 Abraham Lincoln, in a letter to the *Sangamo Journal*, wrote "I go for all sharing the privileges of the government, who assist in bearing its burthens. Consequently I go for admitting all whites to the right of suffrage who pay taxes or bear arms (by no means excluding females)."[10]

For two hundred years women in America had worked alongside men, listened to political discussions, observed the growth of local, state and federal government, and had rarely complained publicly because they were not allowed to vote or hold office. Then in the second and third decades of the nineteenth century the question began to be raised here and there, and by the fourth decade the idea that women should demand a change in their political status was taking shape. Why then? Why not earlier?

Usually when there is a widespread change in the political demands of a large group, it is in the context of a change in the overall environment or in the experience of members of the group. Ideas and social experience coalesce to provide the framework for a social movement. In this case we can see such changes at work.

There was a significant expansion of white male participation in the political process between the late 1790s and 1816. After 1819 constitutional conventions in a number of states adopted changes in suffrage requirements, and by the middle of the 1830s not only had white male suffrage become the norm but politicians were attacked if at any time in their careers they had gone on record as opposing it. The "log-cabin and hard-cider" campaign of 1840, in which the Whigs appealed to a mass audience and organized vast political meetings which lasted for days at a time, reflected these changes. For the first time a presidential candidate appeared on the stump, and women were prominent in the campaign. This "revolution in the habits and manners of the people," as John Quincy Adams described it, included political speaking and pamphleteering on the part of ardent Whig women, and a corresponding effort on the part of the candidates to appeal for female support. Daniel Webster himself, campaigning in Virginia, announced one speech for ladies only, and the *Cleveland Axe* surmised that if women could vote they would "*sweep* Locofocoism from the country in short order." The *Cincinnati Gazette* asserted that "women are the very life and soul of these movements of the people."[11]

Once women had tasted the excitement of partisan politics they were disinclined to give up the fun. In 1856 the new Republican party (which included among its supporters many former Whigs) appealed for women's support, and made much of the participation in the campaign of the candidate's wife, Jessie Benton Frémont.

Activity in political parties was only one of the ways in which American women began to fashion a public role for themselves between 1810 and 1850. The great moral reform movement gave rise to female missionary and tract societies. Humanitarian and philanthropic in intent, these associations also helped women learn how to assume public responsibility. Dorothea Lynde Dix, who carried her campaign for improving conditions of the mentally ill into many state legislatures, was an outstanding example of a woman whose humanitarian concerns carried her directly into politics. Frances Wright was another. As early as 1825 she had proposed to Congress a grand plan for setting aside public land, in a project whose purpose was to abolish slavery. Though she was bitterly attacked for her political views as well as for what was seen as her inappropriate political activity, she nevertheless made influential friends among American politicians and became a model for a handful of young women growing up in the 1820s and 1830s. When the first volume of the *History of Woman Suffrage* appeared in 1887 her picture was its frontispiece.[12]

Emma Willard, Catherine Beecher and Mary Lyon came to public life as a result of their desire to improve educational opportunities for women and to train teachers. Margaret Fuller, transcendentalist and friend of Emerson, was a writer, editor, teacher and journalist. In 1845 she published an important feminist book, *Woman in the Nineteenth Century*, and a few years later she turned up in Italy taking part in the 1848 revolution there.

Also engaged in forging a new role, though in quite a different way, were the young women who provided the labor force for the early textile mills in New England. Somewhat sentimentalized as the "Lowell girls," these women were the first Americans to confront the problems of factory discipline and the new kinds of employer-employee relations which were developing as industrialization proceeded. They, too, took their case to the public, both in print and in early labor agitation. They were the first of what would be an ever increasing number of women in the industrial labor force.

At the same time the antislavery movement was stimulating debate about women's public role. Women who argued for the rights of slaves began to see parallels. "The investigation of the rights of the slave has led me to a better understanding of my own," Angelina Grimké wrote, adding that because all rights grew out of the moral nature of human beings, all human beings should therefore have essentially the same rights.[13]

In addition, women were startled and angered by their reception in the movement itself. Antislavery associations, made up of people dedicated to the idea that Christian principles and the Declaration of Independence should apply to Negroes as well as white men, split over the question of whether women should be allowed to be full-fledged participants in the struggle to end slavery. Men who had argued for years that the Bible should not be used to justify the institution of slavery now resorted to St. Paul for ammunition to keep women in their place.

Similar controversies broke out in temperance conventions, and even in meetings of educational associations where women teachers were denied the right to speak. "The whole land seems aroused to discussion of the province of woman," Angelina Grimké wrote in 1837, "and I am glad of it. We are willing to bear the brunt of the storm, if we can only be the means of making a break in the wall of public opinion which lies in the way of woman's rights, true dignity, honor and usefulness."[14]

As the controversy spread, women began to enter the fray in print. Sarah Grimké responded to the abuse heaped upon her sister and other women lecturers with *Letters on the Equality of the Sexes*, a broad-gauged analysis and critique of the whole female experience in American society, the first such study and still a classic of its kind.

Responses to the Challenge

Since the traditional exclusion of women from public life was being challenged both in theory and in practice, it is not surprising that there was a powerful countereffort to reaffirm women's restricted role, a new affirmation of the idea of "woman's sphere." An increasing number of advice books fell from the newly mechanized printing presses, many of them directed toward reinforcing the view that God and nature had defined woman's role, and that women who tried to change it were a danger to themselves and to society.

Many component parts of this "cult of domesticity" were already familiar in the eighteenth-century definitions of the "lady." Women had long been advised from the pulpit to be submissive to their husbands, and in the seventeenth century John Winthrop had cheerfully diagnosed a woman as mentally ill because she wanted to read and discuss books. What was new in the nineteenth century was the weaving of all these elements together, with the addition of an extraordinary glorification of the role of the mother.

In 1854 young James A. Garfield, then a teacher in an Ohio college, went to hear Antoinette Brown, one of the first women to be ordained in the ministry. His reaction provides an excellent example of the contemporary view of woman:

... there is something about a woman's speaking in public that unsexes her in my mind, and how much soever I might admire the talent, yet I could never think of the female speaker as the gentle sister, the tender wife, or the loving mother. ... The sacred place in my affections which Woman holds would be desecrated by the super addition of the business of public life and a contact with the coarser pursuits of Humanity.

Garfield's fiancee was as much convinced of the theory as he was himself. Just a year later she noted in *her* diary that she wanted "to share his toils—cheer him in his labors with kind and loving smiles and throw around him all the attractions of a sweet home which my poor nature can bestow."[15]

A good many people saw emancipated women as a threat to social order, and there was pressure to close the lid of Pandora's box before it was too late. Press and pulpit reiterated the view of women Garfield expressed, and most men found such views congenial. A few did not. William Lloyd Garrison, for example, could say "I doubt whether a more important movement has been launched touching the destiny of the race, than this in regard to the equality of the sexes," while Emerson wrote in his journal in 1851: "Today is holden at Worcester the 'Woman's Convention,' I think that as long as they have not equal rights of property and right of voting they are not on a right footing." The brothers Blackwell, who married pioneer feminists, shared their wives' work for changing woman's role, as did the venerable Quaker, James Mott. In 1854 Arthur A. Denny, one of the founders of Seattle, offered an amendment to an election bill before the Washington territorial legislature giving the vote to all females over eighteen; the amendment almost passed.[16]

Among women also, the majority accepted the prevailing view of woman's place. Antifeminist prejudices were woven into the culture of the time and were acquired as part of the process of living and growing up in America. Boys learned of their superiority over their sisters—and their sisters learned it as well. Occasionally young women would grow up to question the established ideas but far more often they were successfully socialized into the ideology of the time and grew up to be its defenders.

The First Convention

Though the dissidents were a tiny minority, they were beginning to find each other. In 1848 a small notice in a local paper brought three hundred people from the area, forty of them men, to the Wesleyan Chapel in Seneca Falls, New York to attend a convention "to discuss the social, civil and religious rights of women." This meeting, called by a small group led by Elizabeth Cady Stanton and Lucretia Mott, adopted a Declaration of Sentiments modelled on the Declaration of Independence. First in a long list of charges was the complaint that men did not permit women to exercise the "inalienable right to the elective franchise" (Document 3).

Though the demand that women should be permitted to vote was radical in its implications, the argument was familiar. People who could not vote were being governed without their consent. The Declaration of Sentiments asked only that the Declaration of Independence be followed to its logical conclusion. If rights were given by the Creator was it likely that he discriminated on grounds of sex? Women were one-half the population. If they had no right to vote, the idea of consent of the governed was hollow.

The Seneca Falls meeting marked the formal beginning of a feminist movement in the United States. The Declaration of Sentiments was to become the most significant document in the history of American feminism. In addition to demanding the right to vote, it offered a ringing protest against the entire body of legal, moral, social and economic conditions in which women lived, and demanded change in virtually the whole range of relations between man and woman. In a society in which men were lawmakers and sources of values the simple assertion that "We hold these truths to be self-evident: that all men *and women* are created equal . . ." was potentially explosive.

The Declaration pointed the way to a woman's rights ideology. It described the existing situation in terms of oppression. If married, a woman was dead in the eyes of the law. She could not own property, even her own wages. Divorce laws favored men; women were denied the right to education since all colleges were closed against them. These inequities were not inadvertent but were part of a long-standing pattern: "The history of mankind is a history of repeated injuries and usurpations on the part of man toward woman . . ."

The Declaration dwelt upon injustice. *Any* man, even the most degraded, enjoyed rights denied to *all* women, even the finest. Man protested being forced to submit to laws in which they had no voice, but did not hesitate to subject women to laws in which *they* had no voice. Men had established a double standard of sexual morality so that "delinquencies which exclude women from society are not only tolerated, but deemed of little account in man." Where was justice in all this? Of what value were principles of human justice if they were not applied to both sexes?

The Declaration did not stop with defining grievances; it called for action. Women had been patient under abuse but now they would demand "the equal station to which they are entitled." They were under no misapprehension about the treatment they could expect:

> In entering upon the great work before us, we anticipate no small amount of misconception, misrepresentation, and ridicule; but we shall use every instrumentality within our power to effect our object.

Twelve resolutions provided a program for action. For example, a push for what would now be called "affirmative action":

> He has monopolized nearly all the profitable employments, and from those she is permitted to follow, she receives but a scanty renumeration. He closes against her all the avenues to wealth and distinction which he considers most honorable to himself. As a teacher of theology, medicine, or law, she is not known.

The need for consciousness-raising was recognized:

> *Resolved*, that the women of this country ought to be enlightened in regard to the laws under which they live, that they may no longer publish their degradation by declaring themselves satisfied with their present position, nor their ignorance, by asserting that they have all the rights they want.

The Declaration took account of the effects of male domination on the female personality since men worked " . . . to destory her confidence in her own powers, to lessen her self-respect, and to make her willing to lead dependent and abject life." The drafters wanted equality in sexual mores:

> Resolved, that the same amount of virtue, delicacy, and refinement of behavior that is required of woman in the social state, should also be required of man, and the same transgressions should be visited with equal severity on both man and woman.

Even the Equal Rights Amendment was foreshadowed as the convention resolved that all laws which placed women in an inferior position were "of no force and authority." Except for the resolution calling for the right to vote, all the resolutions passed unanimously.

The Emergence of Leaders

Seneca Falls was the beginning. In the next dozen years a social movement began to take shape centered on the demands for women's rights formulated there. In 1850 a national convention met at Worcester, Massachusetts, and other conventions followed in every year but one before the Civil War. An impressive array of leaders began to emerge in New England, Pennsylvania, New York and the Middle West:

Lucretia Mott (1793-1880) already a giant in the antislavery movement when she joined with Elizabeth Cady Stanton to call the Seneca Falls Convention in 1848. She had long been recognized as a gifted leader among Quakers.

Elizabeth Cady Stanton (1815-1902) headstrong and intelligent, was making a name for herself with cogent arguments before legislative bodies concerned with married women's property laws.

Susan B. Anthony (1820-1906) Mrs. Stanton's chief coadjutor, an indefatigable organizer in the cause of women as well as of temperance and antislavery.

Lucy Stone (1818-1893) who as a student at Oberlin had organized a secret debating society of women, and had gone out to lecture on women's rights in 1847. She was the leading figure in the first national convention in 1850.

Paulina Wright Davis (1813-1876) had first been roused on the subject when she heard a discussion in church upon the impropriety of women speaking in church. She had joined Ernestine Rose in petitioning the New York state legislature for a married women's property act in the 1830s, had organized the Worcester convention in 1850, and then began publishing a monthly periodical, *The Una*, devoted to the cause.

Clarinda I. Nichols (1810-1885) edited a newspaper in Windham, Vermont, in which she published in 1847 a series of articles on women's civil rights. She persuaded a Vermont senator to introduce a married women's property act.

Frances Dana Gage (1808-1884) dated her awakening from her father's remark: "What a pity she is not a boy . . . " The mother of eight children, she petitioned the Ohio legislature in 1850 to omit the words "white and male" from a new constitution.

Hannah Tracy Cutler (1815-1896) student of both theology and law, enrolled at Oberlin as a widow with three children, and was there recruited into Lucy Stone's debating society. In 1851 she had given a series of lectures on women's rights in London.

There were others, but from this group the general profile becomes clear (Document 10). All but Lucretia Mott had been born in the decade 1810-1820; all but Susan B. Anthony were married; most had children. They were all educated, though some primarily by their own efforts. All had been active in antislavery or temperance or both, and most had been alive to the subject of women's rights before the Seneca Falls Convention. As they got to know each other, they became links in the network of female critics of the status quo which was gradually being developed.

Around them a cohesive movement began to take shape. Discussion, debate, and argument fostered the development of a shared ideology, one which pertained not only to overall objectives but also to broad strategy. If there was not yet much in the way of formal organization, a group learning process was underway, and leaders—each with her own local following—were being identified. There was also now deliberate recruitment of new members, and each of these women presented a persuasive model to younger women. Members, objectives, doctrines, leaders, a communications system and heroines: thus the components of a social movement were accumulated.

Each convention, national or local, could report new progress: changes in state laws, legislators converted to suffrage, newspapers joining the fold. By the tenth annual convention in 1860, Susan B. Anthony was able to report a more friendly press and more serious debate. Elizabeth Blackwell had taken a medical degree, Oberlin was fully coeducational, Antoinette Blackwell had achieved her goal of ordination, and the demand for institutions of higher learning open to women was rising. Optimism ran high.

By 1860 women's demands had been articulated, many essentials of a feminist ideology had been developed, and the suffrage movement was a lusty infant. No one, however, had yet devised a strategy to deal with a central political problem. In democratic theory governments are responsive to citizens because legislators fear the ballot box. But what is to make a government responsive to the demands of a group which lacks political power and whose members cannot express their feelings in elections? This is the problem faced by every group outside the power structure trying to get in; one dramatized most recently in the civil rights movement of the 1960s. It was the problem women faced.

To gain access to political power they needed the vote. Men made all the laws: how were they to be persuaded to share their power? Finding an answer to this problem was not a matter for a day or a week, but for years.

Notes

1. J.C. Spruill, *Women's Life and Work in the Southern Colonies,* (Chapel Hill: University of North Carolina Press, 1938), pp. 237-38.

2. Quoted in Alma Lutz, *Susan B. Anthony* (Boston: Beacon Press, 1959), p. 127.

3. C.F. Adams, *Works of John Adams* (Boston: Little, Brown and Co., 1854), vol. 9, pp. 375-377.

4. L.H. Butterfield, ed., *Adams Family Correspondence* (Cambridge: Harvard University Press, 1963), vol. 1, pp. 370, 382.

5. Warren-Adams Letters, Massachusetts Historical Society, Boston, 1917, vol. 1, p. 235.

6. Judith Sargent Murray, "On the Equality of the Sexes," *The Massachusetts Magazine*, March 1790. Though not published until 1790, Mrs. Murray asserted that the essay had been written eleven years earlier.

7. Diary of Elizabeth Drinker, April 22, 1796, Historical Society of Philadelphia, Pennsylvania.

8. See Linda Kerber, "Daughters of Columbia," in *The Hofstader Aegis: A Memorial*, eds., S. Elkins and E. McKitrick (New York: A. Knopf, 1974). Also Sarah N. Randolph, *The Domestic Life of Thomas Jefferson* (New York: Harper and Bros, 1871), pp. 96-99 for the exchange with Mrs. Bingham.

9. This description is drawn from Edward Raymond Turner, "Women's Suffrage in New Jersey 1790-1807," in *Smith College Studies in History*, vol. 1, no. 4, July 1916.

10. Roy P. Basler, ed., *Abraham Lincoln: His Speeches and Writings* (Cleveland: World Publishing Co., 1946), p. 38.

11. See R.G. Gunderson, *The Log Cabin Campaign* (Lexington: University of Kentucky Press, 1957), pp. 4, 8, 73, 121, 127, 135-39, 178-179.

12. Paulina Wright Davis, in *A History of the National Woman's Rights Movement* (New York: Journeymen Printer's Co-operative Association, 1871), p. 9, identifies Frances Wright's early lectures as the beginning of the women's rights movement. She also identifies as pioneers Ernestine Rose, a Polish woman who began in 1836 to lecture on "The Science of Government," "Political Economy," and "Equal Rights of Women," and Mary S. Grove who began lecturing on "Women's Rights" in 1837.

13. Angelina Grimké to Catherine E. Beecher, Letter XII, reprinted in Aileen Kraditor, *Up From the Pedestal* (Chicago: Quadrangle Press, 1968), p. 62.

14. Quoted in Gerda Lerner, *The Grimké Sisters of South Carolina* (Boston: Houghton Mifflin and Co., 1967), p. 183. See Aileen S. Kraditor, *Means and Ends in American Abolitionism* (New York: Random House, 1967), pp. 42-45.

15. Henry J. Brown and Frederick O. Williams, eds., *The Diary of James A. Garfield* (East Lansing: Michigan State University Press, 1967), vol. 1, p. 259. Diary of Lucretia Rudolph, L.R. Garfield Papers, Library of Congress, Washington, D.C.

16. Bliss Perry, *The Heart of Emerson's Journals* (Boston: Houghton Mifflin, 1926), p. 257. T.A. Larsen, "Emancipating the West's Dolls, Vassals and Hopeless Drudges: The Origins of Woman Suffrage in the West," in *Essays in Western History in Honor of Professor T.A. Larsen*, ed., Roger Daniels, (Laramie: University of Wyoming Press, 1971), p. 2.

2

The Making
of a
Movement

> The question of the enfranchisement of
> women has already passed the court of
> moral discussion, and is now fairly ushered
> into the arena of politics, where it must
> remain a fixed element of debate until party
> necessity shall compel its success . . .
> *The Revolution*, vol. 1, no. 1, 1968

Political Developments and Alternatives

By 1860 a social and political movement was taking shape around the
demand for women's rights. It was a small, somewhat beleaguered movement,
whose principal accomplishments had been some changes in state laws
governing married women's property rights and a considerable broadening of
women's educational opportunities. Enfranchisement was only one of the
board spectrum of rights for which women contended, but woman suffrage
was emerging as a clear, easily understood goal around which support could
be mobilized and which could tap the strain of natural rights doctrine in
American thought. But to gain suffrage from male voters women needed a
broad constituency and an effective political strategy.

The movement's natural supporters—women—had proved hard to mobilize.
Male values shaped the culture, and anything which alienated men was apt to
cost women dearly. The "true woman" was supposed to be pious, submissive
and domestic, and many women were frightened when their more adven-
turous sisters began to challenge the taboos of this male-dominated society.
Even women who privately applauded such challenges were often afraid to do
so openly. The challengers therefore faced the twofold task of emboldening
or persuading their potential constituency and then forcing male politicians
to take that constituency seriously.

The legal and educational changes accomplished in the first twelve years
after Seneca Falls were encouraging. Then came the Civil War, and new
complications. Persuaded, over Susan Anthony's objections, to forego
agitation in favor of war work, women contributed in many ways to the
conduct of the war itself. Stanton and Anthony organized the Women's
National Loyal League to press for quick passage of the Thirteenth
Amendment in its 1865 version. Striking an indirect blow for suffrage, they
launched a massive petition campaign with the words: "Women, you cannot
vote or fight for your country. Your only way to be a power in the

government is through the exercise of this one, sacred, constitutional 'right of petition,' and we ask you now to use it to the utmost..." Antislavery senators assured the women that the 400,000 signatures to their petitions contributed significantly to the adoption of the amendment abolishing slavery.[1]

With the ratification of the Thirteenth Amendment the antislavery goal which had brought so many women into public life was achieved. It was not immediately clear where this left women's rights. In May 1865 the Anti-Slavery Society met to hear William Lloyd Garrison argue that the organization could now dissolve. Wendell Phillips disagreed on the grounds that until the freedmen had the right to vote, the society still had hard work to do (*Alternative 1*).

Most women in the society stood with Phillips, partly for reasons of their own. It was clear that black suffrage held out the promise of a Republican South; Mrs. Stanton, for one, understood that woman suffrage could offer no such clear payoff for the party in power. She believed women's best hope, therefore, was to link their cause with that of the freedmen. This, as it turned out, was not quite what Wendell Phillips and the antislavery leadership had in mind. They wanted women's support in their drive for black enfranchisement, but not at the price of supporting woman suffrage. Phillips felt it would be difficult enough to persuade moderate Republicans and Democrats, many of whose states did not permit blacks to vote, without the complication of inducing them also to support the unpopular issue of woman suffrage. Only four antislavery men stood with the increasingly indignant women.[2] Thus began what would become a bitter division among prewar reformers, one which would separate men from women and, in a short time, would split the ranks of women themselves.

Despite Phillips's opposition, Elizabeth Cady Stanton stood her ground and told the first postwar Women's Rights Convention, meeting in New York in May 1866, that women should avail themselves of "the strong arm and blue uniform of the black soldier to walk in by his side, and thus make the gap so wide that no privileged class could ever again close it against the humblest citizen of the republic." Women, she argued, should close ranks with the blacks and antislavery men and appeal for universal suffrage on the basis of natural rights. Members of the convention accepted her reasoning, and constituted themselves the American Equal Rights Association open to men and women, blacks and whites.

The Equal Rights Association was hardly in being when Congress passed and sent to the states for ratification the Fourteenth Amendment, which did not enfranchise the blacks, but instead guaranteed them equal protection of their state's laws, and provided for a reduction in representation if a state denied the vote to male citizens. Not yet alert to any possibilities for themselves in the equal protection clause, suffragists in the Equal Rights Association were incensed by the proposal to add the word "male" to the constitution, and therefore the members undertook to oppose ratification of this amendment. The Republicans campaigned on a platform of ratification of the Fourteenth Amendment in the 1866 congressional elections, and won. They then moved to a firmer position on black suffrage, and began to formulate the Fifteenth Amendment.

That amendment represented a fundamental change in American government. The 1789 Constitution had left the determination of the qualifications of voters entirely to the states. The Fifteenth Amendment limited state options for qualifying voters, forbidding states to deny the right to vote to citizens of the United States on account of race, color or previous condition of servitude. Women's rights advocates saw hope for their cause in this shift, since a single federal amendment would surely be easier to obtain than amendments in all the states. They proposed that the Fifteenth Amendment be drawn to include sex as well as race. Few Republican leaders in Congress, however, were in favor of woman suffrage, and even those who were thought its inclusion at such a critical time might jeopardize their effort to enfranchise black men.[3]

The introduction of the word "male" into the Constitution for the first time in the Fourteenth Amendment and the ratification of the Fifteenth Amendment without mention of sex were the most serious of a series of disappointments (*Alternative 2*). In 1867 the New Jersey legislature, despite Lucy Stone's best efforts, had rejected a suffrage proposal thirty-two to twenty-three. Also in 1867 the New York constitutional convention had proved resistant to the women's arguments. And in the same year a dramatic campaign in Kansas for black and woman suffrage saw the defeat of both propositions, though the women drew nine thousand votes, which represented one-third of the total vote.

Divisions in the Movement

In the midst of these defeats a conflict arose between old friends in the women's movement. Stanton and Anthony on the one hand and Lucy Stone and her husband Henry Blackwell on the other—each surrounded by like-minded friends—began to diverge. Differences centered on a number of issues: how the funds of the Equal Rights Association were to be used; whether men should be welcomed as allies after their apostasy in the case of the reconstruction amendments; and, most important, whether the amendments themselves should be supported despite their failure to include women. In 1869 Stanton and Anthony quietly gathered their supporters into a new organization, the National Woman Suffrage Association. A few months later Stone and Blackwell called a general meeting of women's rights advocates in Cleveland which proceeded to organize the American Woman Suffrage Association, on what they described as a more representative basis. Soon the two groups were vying with each other for the loyalty of state and local suffrage organizations, as well as that of particular individuals. In Massachusetts, the still-powerful Radical Republicans supported the American Association and helped with its funding, apparently fearing the Stanton-Anthony group as a possible center for an independent radical movement.

Though there were a number of abortive efforts to bring the divergent groups together, it soon became clear that their differences were not trivial. One recurrent issue centered on the question of strategy: whether the central focus should be on a national suffrage amendment or whether state-by-state enfranchisement was to be preferred. Both factions accepted the principle of moving forward on both fronts, but in practice Lucy Stone and her associates were inclined to concentrate on the states, while Stanton and Anthony experimented with a number of approaches to national enfranchisement. "We have puttered with State rights for thirty years," Anthony would argue in 1877, "without a foothold except in the territories."[4]

In hindsight it seems clear that underlying conflicts on particular issues were two different philosophies concerning the way a reform movement should operate. The drive for women's rights was taking place in a conservative cultural milieu which historians have characterized as Victorian. In the context of extraordinarily rapid demographic and economic change and accompanying political and ideological conflict, many people were fearful of changes in middle class social arrangements, especially those having to do with the family. While actual changes in women's life experience were being brought about by economic growth, by new educational opportunities, openings in business and the professions, new laws and the like, the ideology of "woman's place" was adamant about the sacredness of home and motherhood and the perceived threat of suffrage to both.

In the simplest terms, Stanton and Anthony were willing to attack this ideology head-on; Stone and Blackwell were more deeply attached to it, and did not want to arouse anxiety among potential supporters (Document 4-a). "It is a settled maxim with me," Elizabeth Stanton wrote, "that the existing public sentiment on any subject is wrong . . ." Her behavior demonstrated this conviction.[5] She travelled about the country lecturing, earned money to educate her children, gave private talks to women in which she urged them to limit the size of their families and demand absolute control over their sexual relationships, ran for Congress to test woman's right to do so, and wrote on a variety of highly controversial subjects. Anthony, for her part, was willing to form alliances with all sorts of people—Democrats, Republicans, third party adherents, the American section of the First International, the National Labor Union, and even, briefly, Victoria Woodhull, if there seemed to be profit to the cause of suffrage. Stanton was a consistent theoretical radical; Anthony was a radical on the level of tactics. Both came to seem shocking to Lucy Stone. In her youth she, too, had boldly challenged social convention, but by the late sixties she and Henry Blackwell found it more profitable to work within the framework of gentility, cooperating politically with their friends among the Radical Republicans in Massachusetts.

In the 1867 Kansas campaign Stanton and Anthony had met a wealthy, eccentric Democrat named George Train, and with his money began, in 1868, *The Revolution*, a paper which in addition to supporting suffrage and equal pay for equal work, discussed practical education for girls, worker's demands, and the movement for an eight hour day. Mrs. Stanton wrote virgorous editorials on marriage, divorce, prostitution, infanticide, the inequality of wealth, and conditions in the slums. In the same year Susan Anthony, rebuffed by the Republicans, took a woman's rights document to the Democratic Convention where at least it was read, though to the accompaniment of jeers and shouts, and died in the Resolutions Committee. Declaring a plague on both Democrats and Republicans Anthony turned to organizing working women and exploring the possibilities of a third party.

When *The Revolution* responded to "many letters" asking if the editors opposed marriage by saying that the editors only opposed the *present system* of marriage, in which "nearly every man feels that his wife is his property, whose first duty, under all circumstances, is to gratify his passions, without the least reference to her own health ... or to the welfare of their offspring," or when Susan Anthony associated with labor unions, Lucy Stone's anxiety mounted. Their once warm friendship began to cool.

The differences between the two groups were dramatically illuminated in the early 1870s when Stanton and Anthony briefly associated themselves with the beautiful, clever and unprincipled Victoria Woodhull who had burst upon the suffrage scene with a memorial presented in person to a fascinated congressional committee, in which she argued that the Fourteenth and Fifteenth Amendments had already enfranchised women.

This argument, initially developed by Francis Minor, a St. Louis attorney, was that the Constitution gave the states the right to regulate suffrage but not the power to prohibit it (Document 4-c). The Fourteenth Amendment confirmed this, he argued, since it provided that "no State shall make or enforce any law which shall abridge the privileges or immunities of citizens of the United States." From this it followed, he believed, that since women were citizens, no state could deny them the vote. Therefore women possessed the right to vote and all state laws providing otherwise were unconstitutional. Needless to say, this was a very appealing idea to women who were realistic about the effort which would be required to attain an additional constitutional amendment, and they welcomed Woodhull to their ranks.

From Mary Wollstonecraft's time antifeminists had argued that sexual license was the inevitable concomitant of women's rights. Frances Wright had been vigorously attacked for her views on marriage. When Woodhull and Claflin's *Weekly* began publishing such statements as: "The time is approaching when public sentiment will accord to women the complete protectorship of their own persons, with the right to choose the fathers of their own children, and hold their relations with whom their hearts may be inclined ..." [August 27, 1870], as well as revelations about a presumed illicit sexual relationship between Henry Ward Beecher and one of his parishioners, what one historian called "the free love storm" broke over the suffrage movement. Timid local groups retreated in panic, while Mrs. Stanton's stouthearted reminders that members of Congress were not discredited in the political arena for their private sexual behavior, only added to the furor.[6] In time Susan Anthony detached herself and Mrs. Stanton from the Woodhull influence, but not before much damage had been done. The

American Woman Suffrage Association (whose president Beecher had once been) maintained a discreet silence, and no doubt the Blackwells were duly thankful they had earlier separated themselves from firebrands who had no more sense than to make such friends.

In any case, the two organizations were destined for twenty more years to go their separate ways. While the American Association worked to persuade state legislatures that they should vote for suffrage amendments and published its excellent and well-financed *Woman's Journal,* Susan Anthony and the National Association gradually became the chief representatives of the movement in the public eye, partly because of the imagination with which she seized every opportunity to dramatize the suffrage demand (Document 4-e).

Political Tests and Experiments

In 1872 the regular Republicans, fearing the inroads of the liberal Republicans, adopted a mild platform plank thanking women for "their noble devotion to the cause of freedom" and welcoming them to "wider fields of usefulness." Anthony seized upon this "splinter" as she called it, as well as upon the $1,000 the party offered her for work among women. She campaigned vigorously for Grant against her sometime friend Horace Greeley.

In the same election, on the theory that the Fourteenth and Fifteenth Amendments *did* enfranchise women, and following the example of an intrepid band of women in Vineland, New Jersey who had first gone to the polls in 1868, Susan Anthony led a group of Rochester women in registering and voting. The idea of course was to be turned away from the polls and then to institute a civil suit which could be carried to the Supreme Court, in the hope of a favorable ruling on Minor's interpretation of the Fourteenth Amendment. Anthony was arrested for her part in the Rochester experiment, and while awaiting trial she made twenty-one addresses on "The Equal Rights of all Citizens to the Ballot" and "Is it a Crime for a Citizen of the United States to Vote?" When she was subjected to a directed verdict of guilty, she responded with a speech calculated to stir the hearts of a generation familiar with Patrick Henry:

> May it please your honor, I shall never pay a dollar of your unjust penalty. All the stock in trade I possess is a $10,000 debt incurred by publishing my paper—*The Revolution*— . . . the sole object of which was to educate all women to do precisely as I have done, rebel against your man-made, unjust, unconstitutional forms of law, that tax, fine, imprison, and hang women, while they deny them the right of representation in the government . . . I shall earnestly and persistently continue to urge all women to the practical recognition of the old revolutionary maxim that "resistance to tyranny is obedience to God." [7]

The fine was never paid.

For technical reasons Anthony's case could not be appealed, but Francis Minor had instituted a case on behalf of his wife when she was refused the right to register which did reach the Supreme Court. In October 1875 in

Minor v. Happersett that body, while affirming that women were citizens, declared that the Fourteenth and Fifteenth Amendments did not enfranchise them (*Alternative 3:* see Document 4-d). That road being closed, the National Woman Suffrage Association returned to a new constitutional amendment as the chief focus of its efforts.

In 1876 Susan Anthony and Matilda Joslyn Gage took the presiding officer at the Philadelphia Centennial celebration by surprise, and proclaimed a Women's Declaration of Rights (Document 4-e). A year later she led a group of women onto the floor of the United States Senate bearing suffrage petitions with ten thousand signatures. The senators, after the standard jokes, referred the petitions to the Committee on Public Lands!

A few members were more serious. In 1878 Senator Aaron Sargent of California introduced the amendment which would finally be ratified in 1920:

> The right of citizens of the United States to vote shall not be denied or abridged by the United States or any state on account of sex.

Once introduced, this amendment formed the basis for hearings, and in 1882 both houses appointed Select Committees on Woman Suffrage which several times reported the amendment favorably. Its only floor consideration came in 1886; after a protracted debate the Senate voted it down thirty-four to six, only forty of seventy-six senators bothering to vote. In an uncharacteristic moment of despair Anthony had noted in her diary in 1883: "It is perfectly disheartening that no member [of Congress] feels any especial interest or earnest determination in pushing this question . . . to all men it is only a side issue."

Social Changes: The Growth of Women's Organizations

While opinion in the Congress moved slowly, American society generally was changing in ways which would ultimately affect the nature and structure of the suffrage movement. The more urban and industrial society became, the less the home was the center of economic, social and political life. Women whose lives were confined to "the home circle," as the phrase went, were cut out of much of the mainstream of the culture. With limited opportunities for higher education, they did not participate in the intellectual movements of the time. Unwelcome in business and the professions, they did not take part in planning the great economic development which was transforming the nation, though a growing number of women were part of the ill-paid labor force which made this development possible. In the contemporary term, women were culturally deprived. Increasingly those who had leisure to contemplate their situation realised their deprivation and undertook to do something about it. The result was a very rapid growth of women's organizations in the last half of the nineteenth century.

Earlier there had been church groups and antislavery societies. After 1870 clubs of all kinds proliferated, springing up as if by spontaneous combustion in big cities, in small towns and even in frontier communities. Their purposes were various: literary studies, community action, civic reform; but whatever the purpose they represented also an effort at self-improvement and self-education.

Among them none was more important to the growth of suffrage sentiment than the Woman's Christian Temperance Union. Begun as a group of praying women trying to use moral power to close saloons, the union in 1876 came under the leadership of one of the most remarkable of nineteenth-century Americans. Frances Willard could inspire ordinary people to extraordinary efforts and then channel those efforts in a common cause. A wide-ranging reformer with a sure feel for the nature of the female subculture of her time, she argued for the ballot as a defense of the home, turning the prevailing image of woman to her own purposes. In time the WCTU would enroll two hundred and fifty thousand members, dedicated to a broad reform program, and providing a channel through which conservative women could be recruited to the suffrage cause. Herself a member of the American Suffrage Association and a close associate of Lucy Stone and Mary Livermore, Willard was also a good friend of Susan B. Anthony. Anthony, who was cautious lest men come to think of suffrage and temperance as interchangeable, nevertheless called on Frances Willard for help in situations—and there were many—when temperance women outnumbered members of suffrage organization.

Though the WCTU was more significant than any of the others in changing women's political behavior (Document 5-a), all the voluntary associations of whatever kind served as training schools in which members learned how to organize and conduct projects, developed skill in public speaking, and articulated a body of interests which women shared. Although by their nature primarily vehicles for middle class women, some clubs (the Women's Educational and Industrial Union of Boston was a good example) made strenuous efforts to cut across class lines and meet the needs of working women of all sorts.

While suffrage gained support as a result of the growth of voluntary associations, the division within the organized movement, meantime, was exhibiting some of the characteristic features of sectarianism. Once a reform movement has divided, forces come into play to perpetuate the division. Communication declines, mutual suspicion increases, bitterness feeds on itself and hostility is reinforced. Favorable information about the other side tends to be discounted or filtered out altogether, while unflattering evidence and unverified rumor find easy acceptance. Such was often the case with this division. Carrie Chapman Catt, who came into the movement in the late eighties, remembered how surprised she has been as a young person who admired them all by "the really quite shocking" feeling of the principals about each other.[8]

But other forces were also at work. There is some evidence that Mrs. Stanton, with her usual broad tolerance for human foibles, urged Susan Anthony to let Lucy Stone go her own way in peace. Certainly the local auxiliaries were often unaware of the causes of the split and, once the

Woodhull storm had blown over, Stanton, Anthony and Stone were equally welcomed in many communities. A good many active women managed to remain on good terms with both factions. On one not untypical occasion a member of the National Woman Suffrage Association, drumming up subscriptions for *The Revolution*, bade her Iowa hostess goodbye a few hours before the next houseguest arrived: a member of the American Woman Suffrage Association in search of subscribers for the *Woman's Journal*.[9]

The Movement Reunites

As time went by new supporters were recruited who knew nothing of the battles of the early seventies. It seemed to them manifestly sensible to pool financial resources and coordinate programs in pursuit of the common goal. Pressure from younger women in both organizations finally forced a reconciliation. In 1890 the two joined to form the National American Woman Suffrage Association, and a phase of suffrage history drew to a close.

There is no doubt that the long rift had led to some confusion and duplication of effort, but whether it seriously delayed the coming of suffrage is doubtful. The two organizations, each following its own philosophy and working within its own capabilities, reached more women and men than either could have done alone. Stanton and Anthony could not have ranged so widely or experimented so freely had they been required to secure Lucy Stone's approval; nor could Stone, had she remained with them, have appealed successfully to the more timid or conservative women whom they frightened. Stone herself had made this point at the time of the break:

> I think we need two national associations for woman suffrage so that those who do not oppose the Fifteenth Amendment, or take the tone of *The Revolution*, may yet have an organization with which they can work in harmony.

She added that "each organization will attract those who naturally belong to it."[10]

The rivalry also kept both sides alert and active. It is hard for organizations, even reform organizations, to avoid the deadening effect of routinization, and easy for the leaders to fall into a groove. During the years of division each side kept a sharp eye on the accomplishments of the other, and was rendered more energetic thereby. The widespread expectation that a unified movement would be able to press ahead more effectively was not immediately realized. Instead, unification was to prove a prelude to a significant decline in organizational vigor.

Though they were not always fully apparent to contemporaries, social changes of far reaching significance to women occurred in the last half of the nineteenth century. The falling birthrate, the increasing level of education, the changing patterns of work and the consciousness-raising of voluntary associations together began to create a "new woman" who was of growing interest to social critics and popular commentators (Document 10). In every part of the country women in various ways were breaking out of their limited sphere to take on more important roles in public and political life. In 1893 Frances Willard and Mary Livermore published an impressive biographical dictionary describing fourteen hundred and seventy women leaders from every state in the union. Annie L. Diggs and Mary Ellen Lease were as well known as any member of the Populist party. Jane Addams was said to be the best known American: the catalog could go on and on. By 1896 there were four suffrage states: Wyoming and Utah which had enfranchised women while they were territories, and Colorado and Idaho where men had gone to the polls and voted for woman suffrage.

Women as a social group had made considerable progress since 1848, but the newly merged National American Woman Suffrage Association had yet to find a strategy for political victory in the populous eastern states or in Congress. In the midst of even wider cultural changes, the next twenty years would be devoted to a search for a winning strategy.

Notes

1. Ida Husted Harper, *The Life and Work of Susan B. Anthony* (Indianapolis: Hollenbeck, 1901), vol. I, p. 238.

2. Ibid., p. 270.

3. The issue of women's rights and the Reconstruction amendments is covered in detail in Susan B. Anthony, Elizabeth Cady Stanton, and Matilda Joslyn Gage, *History of Woman Suffrage* (Rochester: Susan B. Anthony, 1881), vol. II and in Harper, *Susan B. Anthony*. An excellent full-scale scholarly analysis is in progress and will be published by Professor Ellen DuBois of the State University of New York at Buffalo. We are grateful to Professor DuBois for sharing her findings with us before publication. Many of the points made here are hers.

4. Stanton, Anthony et al., *History of Woman Suffrage*, vol. III, p. 66. The relationship between the NAWSA and the Radical Republicans in Massachusetts will be spelled out in Ellen DuBois's book.

5. See sketch by Theodore Tilton in James Parton et al., *Eminent Women of the Age* (Hartford: S.M. Betts and Co., 1869.) p. 360.

6. See Louise Noun, *Strong Minded Women* (Ames: The Iowa State University Press, 1969), pp. 177-192 for a discussion of how this particular series of events affected the suffrage movement in Iowa.

7. Alma Lutz, *Susan B. Anthony* (Boston: Beacon Press, 1959), p. 213.

8. C.C.C. to Edna Stantial, Nov. 17, 1937, Carrie Chapman Catt Papers, Manuscript Division, Library of Congress, Washington, D.C.

9. Noun, *Strong Minded Women*, p. 147.

10. Lutz, *Susan B. Anthony*, p. 169.

3

Turning the Corner 1896-1916

> I do feel keenly that the turn of the road has come . . . I really believe that we might pull off a campaign which would mean the vote within the next six years . . . Come! my Dear Mrs. Park, gird on your armor once more . . .
> Carrie Chapman Catt to Maud Wood Park,
> August 20, 1916

A Period of Preparation

Suffrage historians sometimes pin the label "doldrums" on the years from 1896 to 1910, because after Colorado and Idaho no additional states adopted suffrage for fourteen years, and because the federal amendment appeared to be dead. Close examination of what was going on both within NAWSA and in many local communities shows that beneath the quiet surface the currents were running strongly, and activity which would become increasingly visible by 1910 was already building up.

It was only after a good deal of preparatory labor however, that NAWSA itself showed signs of new vitality. Lucy Stone had died in 1893. Stanton and Anthony lived on into the twentieth century, powerful presences to the end but no longer capable of active leadership. The older generation had been in charge for more than forty years; it is no wonder it took new leaders some time to take firm hold of things.

After the merger of the two organizations, pressure on the Congress had declined. In 1893 Anthony had objected to a decision to meet only alternate years in Washington, saying that "The moment you change the purpose of this great body from National to State work you have defeated its object . . ." but she was out-voted. Yet there was no offsetting increase in effectiveness in the states, and when Carrie Chapman Catt became head of the Organization Committee in 1895, ten states had no known suffrage organization. Nobody knew how many clubs there were, or who their officers were. Morale, confidence and energy seemed to be at a low ebb. Mrs. Catt, sometimes frank to the point of bluntness, told the delegates to the national convention in 1898 that the chief obstacle they faced was not antisuffragism or ignorance or conservatism but the "hopeless, lifeless, faithless members of our own organization."[1] She proposed, and carried out, an intensive organization effort. She inaugurated the idea of work conferences as part of every convention, at which a definite plan of work was given each state, including

24

concrete goals for the coming year. She saw this training of workers as a necessary step if the movement was to become effective. Susan Anthony was impressed, and chose Catt as her successor when she gave up the presidency of NAWSA in 1900.

For the next four years, Mrs. Catt worked hard to transform the loose, unwieldly organization into the kind of tightly knit structure she believed necessary for a major suffrage effort. This work was interrupted by her husband's ill health and subsequent death. Anna Howard Shaw took over as president in 1904 but for all her energy and great talent as an orator, she lacked administrative skill and had little capacity to channel the energy of others. The organization floundered. People paid dues and went to meetings, but little seemed to be happening in the national scene.

The Opposition Organizes

In spite of its problems the movement was potent enough to inspire an increasingly organized opposition (Document 6-b). When the first suffrage agitation had begun, opposition was so universal that no one needed to organize it. It was 1872 before the movement presented sufficient threat to inspire a formal antisuffrage group in Boston. As the suffrage movement grew, formal opposition appeared in twenty states, and in 1911 a National Association Opposed to Woman Suffrage was formed.[2]

Not so open but more politically potent than antisuffrage organizations were the economic groups which organized to oppose suffrage in many state referenda, particularly the trade organizations of brewers and distillers. A typical example of their role in a state campaign was described by the chairman of publicity for the California referendum in 1896:

Ten days before election the fatal blow came. The representatives of the Liquor Dealers' League met in San Francisco and resolved "to take such steps as were necessary to protect their interests. . . ." The following letter, signed by the wholesale liquor firms of San Francisco, was sent to saloon-keepers, hotel proprietors, druggists and grocers throughtout the state:

"At the election to be held on November 3, Constitutional Amendment No. Six, which gives the right to vote to women, will be voted on.

It is to your interest and ours to vote against this amendment. We request and urge you to vote and work against it and do all you can to defeat it.

See your neighbor in the same line of business as yourself, and have him be with you in this matter."[3]

The Liquor Dealers were convinced that women, if they could vote, would bring about prohibition.

By the twentieth century representatives of other business interests with a strong concern for politics were also worrying about what women might do with the vote. Textile manufacturers, for example, envisioned women voters outlawing child labor and supporting an ever-increasing amount of protective legislation for workers. The chief justice of North Carolina, whose insight may have been sharpened by the fact that his son edited the *Textile Bulletin*, was to write later:

> ...suffrage for women is largely a labor movement . . . The Senators who prevented the submission of the suffrage amendment . . . were almost wholly from the New England and South Atlantic states, where the cotton mill owners largely furnished the funds for the campaigns of successful parties . . .[4]

As women became increasingly prominent in all kinds of reform movements, conservative businessmen saw suffrage as one of many "social justice" reforms, all of which they opposed. It was not hard, therefore, for a lobbyist with a specific reason for opposing suffrage to find support among his fellows.

Legislative opposition was also based on the general tendency of politicians to view with alarm any significant change in the rules of the game. In the cities, women were active in municipal reform movements, and showed a disturbing interest in "cleaning up" local government. Congressmen were troubled at the thought of women inquiring too closely into their customary political arrangement, the sources of campaign funds, the uses of patronage and the like. The view of politicians presented in suffrage propaganda was not always a flattering one.

Southern members of Congress shared these general concerns and added a few of their own (Document 6-a). In many cases their opposition appeared to rest on the fear that any change in voting arrangements might upset the existing disfranchisement of black men. Woman suffrage might endanger white supremacy, they argued, and furthermore, approving a federal suffrage amendment would seem to reaffirm the validity of the Fifteenth Amendment, which many southerners hoped was a dead letter. If it were *not* dead, then the validity of grandfather clauses and poll taxes enacted to limit black voting might well be in doubt. The political hierarchies were no more sympathetic than individual members. Major parties in the American system rarely embrace a social reform until it has become widely accepted or unless, as in the case of the Fifteenth Amendment, it will directly increase the party's strength. Before 1912 no leader of either party perceived suffrage as presenting a great moral question, as involving significant public policy, or as conferring political advantage.

Underlying these specific sources of opposition was a vast reservoir of male disquiet, which surfaced whenever women appeared to be making progress toward their goals. The arguments had not changed much since the 1850s. God and St. Paul were still said to have ordained an inferior role for women. It was taken as biologically given that men were rational and women emotional. Women were also said to be too frail for the demands of politics, or in danger of being corrupted by close association with politicians. The sexual division of labor was seen as inherent in nature—and yet in danger of being destroyed if women voted. The downfall of the family was freely predicted, and socialism forecast as outcomes of woman suffrage. Or it was said that women were misled about the importance of the vote. Why should anyone capable of motherhood want so trivial a right? And so on (Document 6-b).

It is no wonder women were frustrated in the face of these contradictory and often irrational arguments. What they perhaps did not understand was that when individuals want to believe badly enough they *will* believe. Almost any argument can appear convincing. There existed a tacit agreement among many men on a range of questions having to do with women and the antisuffragists had no trouble tapping it. The point is not that the arguments were implausible but that they revealed how deep male feeling ran. Just as, for women who believed in it, "suffrage" had come to stand for a wide range of changes in woman's social role, so for men who opposed it "suffrage" meant women in pulpit and courtroom, in operating room, political caucus or board room—all traditional male strongholds. Antisuffrage cartoons revealed unconscious fears: men were pictured in kitchen and nursery harrassed with child care and household responsibilities while their wives went gaily off to public business. A social order hitherto based on male domination and female submission was being challenged.

Unfolding events looked different depending upon one's perspective. Every advance for women marked some change in the lives of men. Every victory for women was a defeat for the men who had opposed change. Women's new and better world of equality was, for some men, a world turned upside down. "Unreasoning male prejudice" was, to the holders, simple social truth (Document 6-b). And to complicate matters further, male solidarity was breaking down, as an increasing number of men were converted to the idea that broadening women's world would benefit both sexes. It is perhaps significant that onlookers jeered men in suffrage parades more vigorously than they did women.

It is easy to understand the panic white people often feel when blacks demand their rights, or the fears of an older generation when the young begin to assert themselves. Such were the fears which pervaded many male sancturaries in 1910, fears which created a wall of opposition to woman suffrage.

Some Changes in Woman's Place

However vigorous and well-organized the antisuffragists might be, the larger environment was increasingly favorable to the "new" women. There was, for one thing, the continued decline in the birthrate. In 1800 the number of live births per thousand women of childbearing age had been fifty-five. By the last decade of the century the figure was down to thirty-three—a forty percent decline. Added to the increased number of public schools, and the longer school day and year, this meant that married women were spending a significantly smaller amount of time and energy bearing and caring for children. With the gradual improvement in household technology and the availability of inexpensive servants, these changes freed a good many middle class women to develop interests outside the domestic sphere.

A second change of vast importance was the increase in the number of college educated women. Dating from the opening of Oberlin to women as well as men in 1833, opportunities for higher education had multiplied rapidly, and though they were a very small proportion of all the adult women in the country, the small group of college graduates were more important as leaders in social change than their absolute number might suggest. Five thousand women took the equivalent of a bachelor's degree in 1900, and each year the numbers grew.

Third, and also of great importance for the society, more and more women were working for pay. The vast majority were low paid, unskilled or semi-skilled, and the largest single group were domestic servants. Women factory workers were beginning to see the ballot as a way of improving their bargaining power.

From among the college graduates, professional women and working women, came a number of significant leaders in a wide variety of social reforms.

At Hull House in Chicago, Jane Addams, Florence Kelley and Julia Lathrop were the center of a group of women who identified and sought to remedy the evils of industrial work. Pushing a factory inspection act through the Illinois legislature, they then supported Kelley for the job of factory inspector. In that position she not only enforced the law, but dramatized the evils of the sweatshop. Margaret Dreier Robins was a key figure in the Woman's Trade Union League, and the league itself took part in a series of important labor disputes. In Kentucky Madeline MacDowell Breckinridge was a leader in a half-dozen social welfare reforms; in Missouri Charlotte Stearns Eliot had a similar history. Both had counterparts in many other states. Middle class women like Grace and Edith Abbott, Josephine Goldmark and Frances Perkins cooperated with working women to tackle a wide variety of industrial problems. From the labor movement itself women like Mary Anderson, Agnes Nestor, Alice Henry, Alzina Stevens and Margaret Haley emerged as leaders. The collective history of all these women (and only a few are named here) has never been written, and it is seldom recognized that they constituted one of the major forces contributing to what has come to be known as the progressive movement. The fact that most of these women were also articulate supporters of suffrage, which they saw as necessary, or at least highly desirable, if they were to achieve their reform goals, gave the whole movement a giant push. Furthermore, a good many male reformers, who found women to be effective allies, were also converted to the suffrage cause.

The interaction between women and progressivism was underlined when the Progressive party in 1912 endorsed suffrage—the first time a party with a real chance of winning an election had done so—and when Jane Addams seconded Theodore Roosevelt's nomination for president on the Progressive ticket. Roosevelt had assured her that he was for woman suffrage without qualification.

As one of a long list of major items on the progressive agenda, suffrage became relatively less radical in the popular eye. With the adoption of direct election of senators and the income tax, railroad regulation and workmen's compensation, and pure food and drug laws, reform itself was becoming respectable. In the states, too, suffrage and progressive legislation went along together.

New Organizational Fervor

"Progressivism" brought a change in the atmosphere of politics, and of the suffrage movement. Young people were attracted to social and political action, and enthusiasm was joined with willingness to cross class lines, study economic questions, and engage in public demonstrations. This energy was evident in the growth of local suffrage groups, and in the formation of new kinds of groups alongside the traditional ones. While NAWSA's National Board did not immediately reflect the change, an increase in membership and the emergence of new leaders took place in many communities. After years of slow growth the suffrage movement was in the process of developing a mass base.

In Massachusetts a group of young women in 1901 had created two important new organizations: the Boston Equal Suffrage Association for Good Government and the College Equal Suffrage League, both aimed at reaching members of the community who had hitherto been indifferent to suffrage. Maud Wood Park, just out of Radcliffe, formed the College Equal Suffrage League. The idea proved so timely that she was soon being asked to help with similar groups in other states.

Meantime the Boston Equal Suffrage Association was experimenting with bold new kinds of campaigning: going door-to-door in Boston in every kind of neighborhood, or sending groups of women on a trolley tour of the state, to make suffrage speeches at every stop along the interurban line. Outdoor meetings, set up spontaneously wherever a crowd could be found, brought the message to people who would never have gone to a suffrage meeting on their own. Timid at first, the women took courage from experience and were soon enjoying themselves as well as recruiting new supporters.[5]

Young American women were increasingly aware of the rise of a militant wing in the English suffrage movement. In 1903 Emmeline and Christabel Pankhurst, members of the Labour Party, had launched the Women's Social and Political Union, and by 1905 they were experimenting with dramatic tactics. After they had heckled candidates for Parliament by demanding that they state a position on woman suffrage, members of the union, when they spit upon policemen attempting to quiet them and organized a protest meeting outside the hall, were arrested and sent to jail. For the first time the English press began to pay considerable attention to the suffrage movement. The lesson was not lost on impatient young Americans, who were themselves engaged in developing new and more colorful tactics.

Harriot Stanton Blatch, daughter of Elizabeth Cady Stanton, had come back to New York after years in England during which she had moved in radical circles. Shocked by the inertia of the traditional suffrage groups, she set about organizing the Equality League of Self-Supporting Women, drawing from a new source (women employed in factories, laundries and garment shops) and using such tactics as open air meetings, silent pickets, women poll watchers, and suffrage parades. She brought Mrs. Pankhurst and other English militants to speak in New York, and was adroit in gaining publicity. In a comparatively short time the Equality League recruited nineteen thousand members.

Inez Milholland exemplified one new style of leader. She had organized two-thirds of the Vassar student body in a college suffrage league before her graduation in 1909. Turned down at a number of law schools, she finally got a law degree from New York University, joined Mrs. Blatch's Equality League of Self-Supporting Women, and divided her time between legislative hearings and suffrage parades on the one hand, and picket lines in the interest of the shirtwaist and laundry worker's strikes on the other. She became a Socialist, and edited a "Department for Women" in *McClure's Magazine*. She was only the most flamboyant of a number of college women who came on the scene in the first decade of the century and added a new dimension to suffrage leadership.

In July 1911 the Philadelphia *Public Ledger* carried a notice that a wagon load of women speakers had appeared on a street corner, adding: "The spectacle of a woman with a wagon for a platform pleading for the use of the ballot was so novel that the audience was quick to respond . . ." Nor was the new wave confined to the eastern seaboard or to big cities. In Boone, Iowa, the state's annual suffrage convention in 1908 was addressed by two English militants. A spontaneous parade followed, and even Anna Howard Shaw, there to represent NAWSA, was carried along by the spirit of the affair and gave an open air speech at the end.[6]

Between 1910 and 1913 campaigns in three states showed what new energy and careful organization could do. The first was in the state of Washington, where Mrs. Emma DeVoe (who had learned her political methods under Mrs. Catt's tutelage) ran a quiet campaign based on carefully planned district-by-district organization. Suffrage won almost two to one, and a wave of enthusiasm spread through the movement.

Even more encouraging was the California campaign which began in the spring of 1911. There women combined every new technique they knew of, making use of automobiles (still something of a novelty), contests, billboards and detailed organization aimed at getting out the vote and insuring a fair election. Money and help came from suffragists all over the country. The key to success, Eleanor Flexner concluded, was close attention to small town and village meetings, parlor talks, and "small groups organized where previously there had been no visible signs of interest in woman suffrage."[7] The California victory, though narrow, was enough. Women could now vote in six western states.

The third major breakthrough came in Illinois where the Equal Suffrage Association, with the help of Progressives in the legislature, put through a bill granting women the right to vote in presidential elections (Document 7-c), a measure which did not require a consitutional amendment. There, too, the organization for the legislative campaign was impressively thorough. For the first time in a state east of the Mississippi (and a large populous state at that), women would be able to vote in presidential elections. Morale rose again.

Internal Changes in The Movement

Members of NAWSA, including some on the National Board, were beginning to demand that a clear-cut political strategy be found to take advantage of what was clearly a new opportunity. Between 1910 and 1916 the board was in turmoil, and experienced considerable turnover. For a time it seemed that the organization might destroy itself through internal conflict.

Two young women who had lived in England and taken part in the militant movement there became a focal point of conflict and eventually precipitated a significant reorganization. Alice Paul and Lucy Burns came back to the United States in 1910, helped initiate the use of new methods in Pennsylvania, and in 1912 offered their services to NAWSA for the purpose of organizing a new drive for a national amendment. The board welcomed them, and dispatched them to Washington as its Congressional Committee. It was not long before they made their presence felt.

Woodrow Wilson, arriving for his inauguration on March 3, 1913 and finding no crowd at the station, was told the people were all watching a suffrage parade. Alice Paul could not have planned it better: crowds in town for the inauguration, rowdies undeterred by the police, troops from Fort Belvoir to the rescue, and indignant congressmen demanding an investigation of the police department for its failure to protect a lawful demonstration, dramatized the suffrage cause.

It was not long, however, before members of the NAWSA board began to recognize some important differences between their own philosophy and that of Paul and Burns. Not only had the two young women organized and raised money for a separate lobbying group which they called the Congressional Union, but they were also ready to operate on a different set of political assumptions. Their English experience led them to believe that effective political action required holding the party in power responsible for policy decisions. Since the Democratic party controlled both houses of Congress and the presidency, they reasoned that all Democrats, those who had supported suffrage as well as those who had opposed it, should be held responsible if no action was taken on the suffrage amendment. They proposed to organize women to oppose Democrats in all the suffrage states.

NAWSA had always held to the view that in the American Congress men of both parties would be needed to make up two-thirds in each house, and had therefore insisted on a nonpartisan policy. Suffragists who had worked actively for the Progressive party had been criticized on just this ground.

Paul and Burns failed to understand the essential difference between the English parliamentary system and the United States system. In England the executive had a working majority in Parliament, party discipline was strong, and Parliament could grant the vote to women by a simple legislative act. In the United States the achievement of woman suffrage required that both houses of Congress pass a proposed amendment by a two-thirds vote and that the legislatures or special conventions in three-quarters of the states approve it. Furthermore, party discipline is notoriously weak in this system, and when most measures pass legislatures they are approved by coalitions comprised of members from both of the major parties. Suffrage needed every legislative friend it could find, and it made little sense to oppose supporters in the name of a principle—party responsibility—which was not understood in American politics.

At the 1913 convention, after much discussion, the NAWSA board withdrew its support from Paul and Burns who went their own way thereafter, first in the Congressional Union, then in the National Woman's Party. For the second time the suffrage movement was divided. Few long-lived reform movements escape factionalism, and when splits occur they are apt to separate the radical from the relatively conservative, the venturesome from the cautious, and are likely to revolve around questions of strategy and tactics. This new division was reminiscent of the earlier cleavage between the National and the American associations. Then Lucy Stone and the Bostonians had emphasized moderation, and had tried to avoid extreme actions that might antagonize friends and neutrals. Stanton and Anthony had been prepared to press ahead, letting the chips fall where they might. Now the NAWSA had fallen into comfortable and conservative ways, and was flanked on the left by the more militant Congressional Union.

Events had outrun the leaders of the NAWSA. While new life was stirring in many states, and the Congressional Union was generating excitement in Washington, the board appeared to be plodding along with no clear political strategy. Discontent within the organization was exacerbated by controversy over the board's decision to support a new constitutional amendment, the so-called Shafroth-Palmer amendment, which would have thrown the suffrage issue once again back to the states. On March 19, 1914, for the first time in the twentieth century, the federal amendment was brought to a vote in the Senate, and overwhelmingly defeated. Of the sixty-nine members voting, thirty-four opposed. A roll call in the House on January 12, 1915 was similarly discouraging: yeas 174, nays 204. Discontent came to a head in 1915 after the defeat, despite excellent and imaginative campaigns, of constitutional amendments in four crucial eastern states. Many members of NAWSA called for Carrie Chapman Catt to take the presidency.

In 1887, as a talented young widow with some legal training and experience in education and journalism already behind her, Carrie Chapman had joined the Iowa Woman Suffrage Association. Within two years she was organizing all over the state, and in 1890 Iowa had sent her to the national convention. Her marriage the following year to George Catt had taken her first to Seattle and then to New York, but not out of suffrage activity. She campaigned in South Dakota, Colorado and Idaho, winning in the latter two states. In Idaho she first experimented with an organization based on election districts. She next headed the Organization Committee of NAWSA, and then was president for four years. During the period immediately after her husband's death she had spent a good deal of time organizing the International Suffrage Alliance, and then had returned to New York where she organized the Woman Suffrage party, and began preparing for the referendum which finally came in 1915. In the meantime, methods she had helped to develop contributed to the victories in Washington, California, and Illinois. When the 1915 campaign in New York got forty-two percent of the vote, she had at once launched the next campaign aimed at 1917.

It was this record which led the discontented members of NAWSA to fix their hopes on Mrs. Catt. At the 1915 convention she was persuaded to take the presidency, on the condition that she could choose her own board. She went to work at once to turn NAWSA into a tightly organized, effective force. Now both suffrage organizations were ready to campaign seriously for a national amendment.

Moving Towards a National Amendment: The Election of 1916

The two groups approached the task with different philosophies, and as time went by the divergence would grow. Under Mrs. Catt's leadership, NAWSA would depend upon a high degree of organizational coherence; a close relationship between local, state and national workers, a mass base, careful, low-key lobbying, and ladylike behavior (Document 7-e). The Congressional Union also believed in organization, and it tried to develop a base in the country, especially in the suffrage states. But, in addition, Alice Paul believed in dramatic action, the symbolic gesture, headlines, and in a small, disciplined group of activists. As the union moved further in this direction, NAWSA would take pains to separate itself from its flamboyant activities, and especially to keep the distinction clear in the minds of congressmen.

It is hard now to avoid concluding that the existence of the militant group was important. The temper of the times called for a vigorous pursuit of the goal. Once again, as in the 1868 division, the two groups stimulated each other. Indeed, the challenge from the Congressional Union was part of the stimulus which led to Mrs. Catt's election, and for that reason NAWSA owed the union an unacknowledged debt.

With the Congressional Union and NAWSA both at work the militants could press ahead with shock tactics, while the more conservative group could develop its careful organization based on congressional districts. It was a good one-two punch, as events in 1916 would demonstrate.

That was an important year for woman suffrage. In June NAWSA organized a giant parade to the Republican National Convention being held in Chicago. On a cold, windy, rainy day ten thousand women marched to the convention hall and the *New York Times* reported that some politicians felt this was "the pluckiest thing they ever knew women to do." The Republicans came out for suffrage but in a disappointing states' rights plank. They "recognized the right of each state to settle this question for itself." When the Democrats met in St. Louis, delegates walked to the convention hall through streets lined with women wearing yellow sashes and carrying yellow parasols to remind them of the suffrage issue. After an acrimonious floor debate the Democrats, too, came out for suffrage "state, by state, on the same terms as men."

Carrie Chapman Catt responded by calling an emergency convention to meet in September to which she invited both presidential candidates (Document 8-e). Wilson came and, using notes supplied to him by Alice Stone Blackwell, declared his support for suffrage but added ambiguously "we will not quarrel in the long run as to the method of it." Charles Evans Hughes, the Republican candidate, did not accept the invitation but had already endorsed suffrage by federal amendment. Both parties were beginning to contend for the suffrage votes that had gone to the Progressive party in 1912.

During this convention state presidents and officers of the national association met in secret to hear what would come to be called Mrs. Catt's "Winning Plan." The essence of the plan was that suffragists should move forward on *all* fronts, and each state was given responsibilities depending on its particular status. The eleven full suffrage states and Illinois were to get resolutions from their legislatures memorializing the Congress to submit the federal amendment. In others, referendum campaigns were the task at hand; in some states, campaigns for presidential suffrage, and in the South campaigns for primary suffrage—all aimed at increasing the number of electoral votes which women could influence. Representatives of thirty-six state associations signed a compact to carry out these plans and to keep them secret until they revealed themselves in action. Insofar as possible, the opposition was to be caught napping (Documents 7-a, 7-b, 7-e, and 8-a).

As for the federal amendment, work in Washington was to be organized at a new level of intensity. Just before the Atlantic City convention Mrs. Catt had written to Maud Wood Park:

> I do feel keenly that the turn of the road has come . . . I really believe that we might pull off a campaign which would mean the vote within the next six years if we could secure a Board of officers who would have sufficient momentum, confidence and working power in them . . .
>
> Come! My dear Mrs. Park, gird on your armor once more . . .[8]

That Atlantic City convention gave the National Board—Carrie Chapman Catt's board—authority to direct all the activities of the organization. A million dollar budget was authorized and Mrs. Park and quite a few others did "gird on their armor" and move to Washington for the duration of the struggle.

When Woodrow Wilson surveyed his prospects for reelection in 1916 it was clear that his best hope lay in attracting the votes of many citizens who in 1912 had cast their ballots for Theodore Roosevelt. Accordingly, under his aggressive leadership, the Congress that summer had adopted a number of measures which progressives considered a test of his commitment to their position, especially the Keating-Owen Child Labor Bill. Accordingly, too, he had gone to the NAWSA convention and made his tantalizing statement, opening the door to his eventual support of the federal amendment.

As in 1914, the Congressional Union took the position that since the Democrats had controlled the government for four years *all* Democrats must be opposed (Document 7-f). NAWSA held to its careful bipartisanship, supporting its friends in either party (Document 7-g). With war going on in Europe, peace was a major issue, and on a platform of peace and progressivism Wilson went to the country, polling nearly three million votes beyond what he had received in 1912.

The *New York Times* postelection analysis indicated that women voters had helped to swell this number and had contributed significantly to his victory in California, Idaho, Utah and Arizona. The Woman's Party effort to persuade women to vote against all Democrats had not, apparently, hurt the president very much except in Illinois.[9]

The immediate tactics of the two suffrage organizations had pulled in opposite directions. The failure of the Woman's Party tactic was not surprising since it was based on an erroneous conception of the American political process. Even though its objective was Quixotic, however, the campaign contributed to the growing momentum of the suffrage movement. While the Congressional Union in *The Suffragist* of November 11, 1916 asserted that "the Democratic campaign in the West consisted almost entirely of an attempt to combat the Woman's Party attack," other suffragists were content to give women credit for helping Wilson win, and to let all politicians draw the obvious lesson. Women now voted in states totalling nearly a hundred electoral votes. Candidates had to take notice.

If the *New York Times* is any test, the press, too, was taking increasing notice. From December 1915 to March 1916, only six suffrage stories appeared on the first five pages of the *Times*, and many that did appear were printed along with engagement, marriage, birth and death notices. By July coverage began to pick up, and two and three column articles replaced the earlier brief paragraphs. By late summer editorials and letters to the editor appeared in considerable numbers, including a protracted argument over the right of the federal government to impose woman suffrage on states which had previously defeated state constitutional amendments.[10]

The Sixty-fourth Congress met on December 4, 1916 to hear President Wilson read his message to Congress. Now safely reelected, he did not mention woman suffrage. While he spoke representatives of the Congressional Union seated in the gallery quietly unfurled a large banner: "Mr. President, What Will You Do For Woman Suffrage?" The press reported that after a moment's pause he continued reading, but it was a question that neither Wilson nor the American nation could sidestep much longer.[11]

Four more years of hard work lay ahead for suffragists, but by the end of 1916 the corner had been turned. The ideological and political spectrum had shifted to the left, and in the process woman suffrage had been legitimized in the minds of many Americans. It was rapidly picking up support among women and men in all parts of the country.

After a period of stagnation, new energies and new tactical ideas emerged within the movement and precipitated a division. The new organization, modelled to some extent on that of the English militants, had found its way to new and dramatic tactics.[12] Its emergence, its vigor, and its tactics all served to challenge the National American Woman Suffrage Association and led to its reinvigoration. Though neither organization had much use for the other, they supplemented one another very well. In the atmosphere of progressivism the question was no longer whether women would have the vote in the United States, but only when.

Notes

1. Mary Grey Peck, *Carrie Chapman Catt* (New York: H.W. Wilson, Co., 1944), p. 96.

2. Eleanor Flexner, "Who Opposed Woman Suffrage," chapter 22 in *Century of Struggle* (Cambridge: Harvard University Press, 1958), is a careful and balanced account upon which we draw here.

3. Ida Husted Harper, *Life and Work of Susan B. Anthony*, vol. II, pp. 886-87. Carrie Chapman Catt and Nettie R. Shuler in *Woman Suffrage and Politics* (New York: Charles Scriber's Sons, 1923) detail the charge that brewers and distillers were, early and late, busy opposing suffrage. Such a view had been axiomatic among suffragists for many years, but gained unexpected corroboration when a Senate investigation in 1918, examining alleged pro-German activity among brewers, turned up convincing evidence that these suspicions were more than justified. See U.S., Congress, Senate, Subcommittee on the Judiciary, "Brewing and Liquor Interests", 65th Cong., 1st sess., vol. I.

4. Walter Clark, "Woman Suffrage as a Labor Movement," *American Federationist* 26 (May 1919): p. 392.

5. See Sharon Hartman Strom, "Leadership and Tactics in the American Woman Suffrage Movement: A New Perspective from Massachusetts," forthcoming in the *Journal of American History*.

6. See Harriot Stanton Blatch, *Challenging Years* (New York: G.P. Putnum's Sons, 1940), pp. 91-242. Caroline Katzenstein, *Lifting the Curtain* (Philadelphia: Dorrance and Company, 1955), pp. 46-47. Louise Noun, *Strong Minded Women* (Ames: The Iowa State University Press, 1969), pp. 246-247, and the *Woman's Journal*, 1905-1910 for evidence of the growing influence of English militant methods in the American suffrage movement. Enthusiastic crowds turned out to hear Mrs. Pankhurst, the leader of the English militants, in New York in 1909 and in Boston in 1910.

7. Flexner, *Century of Struggle*, p. 256

8. Carrie Chapman Catt to Maud Wood Park, August 30, 1916, Maud Wood Park Papers, Schlesinger Library, Radcliffe College, Cambridge, Massachusetts.

9. See *New York Times*, Nov. 12, 1916. The analysis is based on observations of local politicians and correspondents; no survey data of the kind which we might have now was available. The only place where women's vote could be accurately measured was Illinois (since women there could vote only for president). In that state women voted more heavily for Charles Evans Hughes, the Republican candidate, than did the men.

10. We are indebted to an unpublished paper by Myla Taylor, Duke University student, for this information.

11. Inez Haynes Irwin, *The Story of the Woman's Party* (New York: Harcourt-Brace, 1921), pp. 185-86.

12. It is important to note that woman suffrage as an international movement had spread widely since New Zealand enfranchised its women in 1893. Australia,

Austria, Canada, Czechoslovakia, Denmark, England, Finland, Germany, Hungary, Ireland, Mexico, Norway, Poland, Russia, and Scotland all had woman suffrage before 1919. See Ross Evans Paulson, *Women's Suffrage and Temperance* (Glenview, Illinois: Scott-Foresman, 1973) for the most recent discussion of the international suffrage movement.

4

Victory: 1917-1920

The right of citizens of the United States to vote shall not be denied or abridged by the United States or by any state on account of sex . . .

Nineteenth Amendment to the Constitution

Winning Plans

For suffragists, scattering from the NAWSA emergency convention to pick up their assigned tasks or gathering in intense conference around Alice Paul at the "Little White House" on LaFayette Square, the fall of 1916 was an exciting time to be alive. Suffrage was suddenly a major issue; newspapers and magazines were full of it, the environment was more accepting than it had ever been, four million women in eleven states could now vote, and members of both organizations were in fine fettle. Women were increasingly exhilarated by the experience of concentrated, demanding work for a high cause, one which was at last making visible progress. An English militant could have been speaking for them all when she wrote: "All the time, watching, attacking, defending, moving and counter-moving! . . . how glorious those . . . days were! To lose the personal in the great impersonal is to live!"[1] For many women the suffrage movement gave a meaning and force to life that would be remembered with keen nostalgia in later years.

The essence of Mrs. Catt's "Winning Plan" was careful coordination of work in the states with lobbying in Washington. In order for women in the congressional districts to do their job, they were supplied with a steady flow of precise information, along with constant reminders to send letters of appreciation to every member of Congress who did anything to help the cause. They were responsible for building every kind of pressure from home: resolutions of all sorts, letters from politically active men, news of mass meetings—whatever they could drum up. The flow of information from Washington required a major effort at that end. Mrs. Park described what she saw when she arrived to join the Congressional Committee:

> . . . file cases holding . . . 531 portfolios, 96 for the Senate and 435 for the House . . . provided . . . all the known data about a senator or representative. There were printed sketches of his life; there were facts supplied by our members in the state about his personal, political, business and religious affiliations; there were reports of interviews . . . there was everything that could be discovered about his stand on woman suffrage and more or less about his views on other public questions . . .[2]

From time to time groups of women from individual states would journey to Washington at their own expense to add their efforts to those of the regular members of the NAWSA Congressional Committee. In January 1917, for example, twenty-nine women arrived from sixteen states. Mrs. Catt's later judgment was that no group ever came to know the inside of Congress as suffragists did.

The Congressional Union deployed smaller numbers in its lobbying effort, but these members were equally diligent—walking the corridors of the House and Senate office buildings by day, and gathering in the evening to exchange information and plot the next step. The Congressional Union also kept full and careful files and sought to use its information in much the same way as did NAWSA.

Although the two groups made similar organizational preparations for lobbying they had different self-images. This was reflected to some extent in the manner in which they conducted their congressional activities. Mrs. Park was concerned with finding just the right woman to make a favorable impression on the member being interviewed. She always sent a woman from a man's own region if possible, recognizing the difficulty a New England woman might have, for example, with a congressman from Georgia. She thought on balance her most successful lobbyists were women from the Middle-West, middle-aged, and "rather too dressy," but "possessed of much common sense and understanding of politics in general, as well as of the men from their districts." They impressed the members, she thought, as substantial citizens of the type who had great weight with office holders.[3]

Congressional Union women did not pride themselves on diplomacy; rather the contrary:

> Here was an army of young Amazons who looked them [congressmen] straight in the eye, who were absolutely informed, who knew their rights, who were not to be frightened by bluster, put off by rudeness, or thwarted either by delay or political trickery. They never lost their tempers and they never gave up . . . They were young and they believed they could do the impossible . . .[4]

There was a measure of fantasy in this description, and doubtless the constant emphasis upon the youth and vigor of Congressional Union women contributed to the friction between the two groups. Neither Mrs. Park in her late thirties nor Mrs. Catt in her fifties felt themselves ready to be put out to pasture.

NAWSA was by now the largest voluntary organization in the country. Two million women, slowly being organized along lines of political jurisdictions, learning the ways of politics, were beginning to make their weight felt. A conference set up to train local people for more effective work in their congressional districts gave evidence of a sense of growing confidence when it adopted a resolution to the effect that if the Sixty-fifth Congress should fail to submit the federal suffrage amendment before the 1918 election, the association would "select a sufficient number of Senators and Representatives for replacement" to assure passage by the Sixty-sixth.[5]

The Texas congressional chairman was an example of the new breed NAWSA was developing: she arrived in Washington well acquainted with the situation in most Texas districts, and went off at once for interviews on Capitol Hill. Coming back to Suffrage House at night she remarked of one Texas member, "There is nothing we can do but retire him. That is what we will have to do."[6]

Every new achievement in the states added to the stock of "good news" the congressional committee found so helpful in Washington. In one eight month period in 1917 the number of electoral votes dependent in part on women jumped from 91 to 172. Good news indeed.[7]

With the help of Wilson's close friend Helen Hamilton Gardener ("a woman of genius," Maud Wood Park wrote, "who was to teach me almost everything of value I came to know during those years in Washington") NAWSA kept up a steady pressure on the president. Mrs. Gardener was infinitely polite and diplomatic.

Not so the Congressional Union. Convinced that Wilson could and should do more to push the Congress, on January 10, 1917, pickets appeared at the White House bearing banners with such slogans as MR. PRESIDENT! HOW LONG MUST WOMEN WAIT FOR LIBERTY? As Wilson went out for his afternoon drive, fine words from his own writings on democracy were waved before him. On inauguration day a thousand women walked slowly round and round the executive mansion.

The president whom they were trying to recruit to their cause was, by this time, almost wholly preoccupied with the implications of the European War for the United States. In January he had laid before the Congress his "Peace Without Victory" message describing the kind of settlement he hoped would be reached among the warring powers. His grand hope was that the United States, from a position of strict neutrality, would be able to bring both sides to the peace table, and lead them to a new era in international relations. In the event, he got not peace but war. By the end of February the Germans had made it clear that they were determined to sink every ship in the war zones they could, neutral and belligerent alike. This, Wilson felt, the United States could not tolerate. This new Congress was summoned into special session to receive the president's war message, and on April 6 it declared war on the Central Powers. There were many pacifists among suffrage workers, and these watched with pride as Jeannette Rankin of Montana, the first woman to be elected to the Congress, cast one of the fifty votes against the war resolution. There was also some dismay as other suffrage leaders counted the possible cost of being identified with Miss Rankin's presumed lack of patriotism.

The war changed the situation in which the suffrage campaign was conducted. Mrs. Catt had foreseen the possibility that war would come, and in February the Executive Council of NAWSA, after long debate, had decided to pledge service to the government if war should come, but decided also that it would continue the suffrage effort without relaxation. The National Woman's Party, which now encompassed the Congressional Union, decided in convention that while individual members could do as their consciences dictated, the organization as such would take no part in war work. It would continue to work for woman suffrage and for that alone, believing that in so doing it would "serve the highest interest of the country."[8]

Militant and Effective Tactics

Picketing of the White House by the Woman's Party had proceeded peacefully at first, but in the summer of 1917 the placards became more provocative (Document 8-b). The president was called "Kaiser Wilson" and Russian envoys from the Kerensky government arriving at the White House were greeted with signs warning them that there was no real democracy in the United States. Onlookers were provoked, skirmishes broke out, and in time arrests began. More than two hundred women were arrested, and ninety-seven sentenced to jail for "obstructing the sidewalk." The newspapers reported every incident, usually on the front pages. In jail the women protested their miserable conditions and rough handling, demanded to be treated as the political prisoners they felt themselves to be, and finally went on a hunger strike. Embarrassed and outmaneuvered, the administration dropped the charges and released the prisoners.

The women of NAWSA and many of their friends in Congress were sure these militant tactics hurt the movement and slowed the progress of the amendment. The Woman's Party insisted that the reverse was true, and took credit for the favorable report which came from the Senate Committee on Woman Suffrage on September 15, and for the long-delayed appointment of a House Committee on Woman Suffrage on September 24, accomplishments which NAWSA thought "we came very near losing because of their activities."[9]

Probably the militant tactics did more good than harm. Nervousness about what the radical women might do next encouraged both Congress and the president to make concessions and to embrace the more conservative suffragists as the lesser evil. The sequence here, as elsewhere, illustrates the usefulness of a radical faction in a reform movement. But for the rivalry and complementarity of the two, the federal amendment might have been delayed for years, though neither faction was prepared, then or later, to recognize the contribution of the other.

While the country slowly geared itself to fight a war, suffragists in New York were busier and better organized than ever before. In November the suffrage referendum there carried by an impressive margin of one hundred thousand votes. This was dramatic progress, especially at a time when much energy of activist women was going to war work. When the Sixty-fifth Congress met for its regular session in December, women in Washington could tell the difference the New York referendum result had made in their reception on the Hill.

Almost immediately the House adopted the prohibition amendment, which removed another obstacle. The liquor interests had long feared that women voters would enact prohibition; if prohibition was coming anyway there was no reason to waste time and effort fighting woman suffrage. Maud Wood Park noted that "Many wet opponents . . . felt their chief reason for objection was gone."[10]

President Wilson was coming to believe that both party necessity and his own position as an international leader required him to support a federal suffrage amendment (Document 9-a). On January 4, 1918 the *New York Times* reported that Theodore Roosevelt had written the Republican National Committee urging that everything possible be done to persuade Republican congressmen to vote for the amendment, and suggesting that a woman from each suffrage state be added to the National Committee itself. Five days later Wilson advised a delegation of Democrats to vote for the amendment "as an act of right and justice to the women of the country and of the world." On the same day in a private letter he said that though he hesitated to volunteer advice to congressmen, when anyone asked he advised them to vote for the amendment.[11]

In the first issue of *The Revolution* in 1868 Elizabeth Cady Stanton had foreseen a time when party necessity would force men to vote for woman suffrage. That time had finally arrived. As each additional state adopted suffrage, national party leaders became more respectful. The women's vote had become a factor in many election calculations.

On January 10, 1918 the House of Representatives witnessed one of those dramas of which myths are made: galleries packed with tense, waiting women; sick men brought from their beds to vote; a New York congressman leaving the deathbed of his suffragist wife to cast his ballot. Only six members failed to vote (or to be paired)—itself an indication of how important the amendment had become since 1915 when forty-one had failed to be recorded. When the roll call ended there were 274 yeas and 136 nay votes—the necessary two-thirds had finally been achieved.

Thirty-three New Yorkers had voted yes, twenty-two more than in 1915. Eighteen percent of the southern representatives now voted for the bill; two percent had voted yes in 1915. And while ninety percent of the men from suffrage states had voted yes, so had half those from nonsuffrage states, a gain from the thirty-six percent in 1915. While the increase in the number of suffrage states was the most vital factor in victory, the increase in suffrage sentiment in nonsuffrage states was also very helpful.

As women poured out of the galleries a Woman's Party member from Massachusetts struck up the doxology. The marble halls reverberated to the sound of "Praise God from which all blessings flow . . ." and for a few minutes NAWSA and Woman's Party members sang in harmony.

Battle for the Senate

God's blessing did not flow all at once, however, for there was still the Senate to be conquered, and that body proved itself capable of resistance to both popular and presidential pressure. Six year terms protected senators from the immediate impact of public opinion, and though direct election had been in effect since 1913, one-third of the members still held their seats courtesy of a state legislature. Ten prosuffrage senators had died during the Sixty-fifth congress. And then there was the South. Southern senators from one-party states had less to fear from competition at election time, and more dread of the possible consequences of a federal amendment. Southern women were flocking to the cause: Senator Simmons from North Carolina, for one, heard often from his daughters on the subject, but his vote was not changed. Many southern women came, bearing petitions and other evidence of the change of opinion back home. A petition signed by one thousand of the country's "best known" men added to the pressure on the Senate.

Still NAWSA's careful check list indicated that two additional votes were needed for the required two-thirds. The women praised the courage of Louisiana Senator Ransdell who supported suffrage as a matter of justice, while admitting that many of his constituents did not agree, and gave grudging admiration to McCumber of North Dakota who said he would vote for the amendment despite his own convictions, because his state had granted women the vote.

During the winter and spring of 1918 both suffrage organizations tried to recruit two more senators. On May 22 Wilson said ruefully that he had done everything he could think of, to no avail. Mass meetings were organized throughout the country, and on July 13 a massive demonstration was mounted on Boston Common. Conventions of the American Federation of Labor and the National Education Association among others called for action.

By July 17, in response to Mrs. Park's urgent plea, 554 resolutions had come in from a variety of organizations. Indiana alone supplied 120, and only Delaware and Georgia failed to send any.[12] The Democratic National Committee voted unanimously to support the amendment; the Republicans had already done so.

In August the Woman's Party once again took to the streets, and a new round of arrests began. In September the pickets added a new twist—burning Wilson's speeches before the White House gate, once again accusing him of hypocrisy, despite his by now vigorous efforts on behalf of the amendment. (Between June and August he made personal pleas to eight antisuffrage senators.) Twice the Senate had seemed ready to vote; twice the chairman of the Woman Suffrage Committee, Senator A.A. Jones, had withdrawn the amendment rather than risk defeat. Then, on September 26, he moved to take it up.

After five days of debate in which all the old arguments were once again rehearsed, the president took the extraordinary step of appearing in person to plead for a favorable vote. He argued that the suffrage amendment was vital to "the winning of the war and to the energies alike of preparation and of battle." It was also, he said, "...vital to the right solution of the great problems we must settle . . . when the war is over."[13] Other members of his party were saying, not so publicly, that the fall elections might well turn upon the passage of the amendment. Neither the president nor the prosuffrage Democrats prevailed; the roll call was taken and still two votes were needed for a two-thirds majority (*Alternative 4*).

The *New York Tribune* reported that Republicans expected to gain Progressive votes in November as a result of the intransigence on the part of southern Democrats, and suggested that both houses of Congress might change hands as a result. It thought the voters would rebuke senators who had voted "no," since the United States "will not long support a Senate that insists upon being more reactionary and less progressive than the British House of Lords." The *New York World* could "find no evidence of consistency or principle," saying that the adverse vote "represented personal prejudice rather than adherence to any known theory of government." David Lawrence writing in the *Evening Post* reported that northern and western Democrats were indeed worried about the election. "It is truly an extraordinary situation," he said with some wonder, "and woman is at the bottom of it all."[14]

On October 25 Wilson again took an unusual step when he asked the voters to return a Democratic Congress to help him end the war and win the peace. When the dust settled after the election the Republicans had gained twenty-five seats in the House, and six in the Senate. This election has sometimes been interpreted as a sharp rebuke to the president, but one of the country's leading political scientists assessed the change, at the time, as about normal for off year elections.

Republicans gained six seats in Ohio, four each in Indiana and Kansas, three each in New York, Pennsylvania, Missouri and Nebraska, two in Colorado, and one each in California, and West Virginia. All but five of these were suffrage states. However, Democrats also defeated Republicans for particular seats in New York, New Jersey, Pennsylvania, California, Nevada, and Oklahoma, so generalization is impossible. The chances are that local situations were as important in many races as national issues.[15]

NAWSA had lived up to its threat to select recalcitrant senators for defeat, and had chosen four, two from each party, as objects of special campaign efforts. Somewhat to their own amazement, by excellent organization of women in both states, Republican Senator Weeks in Massachusetts and Democratic Senator Saulsbury in Delaware were defeated. The other two, Moses of New Hampshire and Baird of New Jersey were returned, but with diminished majorities. Unless death once again took off prosuffrage senators, the precious two votes were now assured.

But the women were taking no chances. After yet another failure to get a favorable vote in the lameduck session of the Sixty-fifth Congress (Document 9-b), they turned all their energy toward making sure of the Sixty-sixth (Document 9-c). Resolutions again poured in: twenty-four state legislatures asked the Congress to submit the amendment.

Wilson, in Paris for the peace talks, continued to urge support upon hesitant Democrats. The fall elections had added three more full suffrage states and six more presidential suffrage states, as well as bringing primary suffrage in Arkansas and Texas. Women could now vote for presidential electors in thirty states for a total of 339 electoral votes. The "Winning Plan" was working. The House, with 117 new members, passed the amendment for a second time, this time by a vote of 304 to 89. Of all the new men voting, only six voted no! Two hundred and twenty-four of those voting yes came from suffrage states, and eighty from nonsuffrage ones. Thirty percent of the southerners were now voting yes, a significant change in sentiment since the first roll call in 1915. All six Arkansas congressmen, three of four from Florida, and ten of seventeen from Texas swelled the southern contribution. Only Mississippi and South Carolina remained solidly "no."

Then, at long last, came June 4 when the Senate was to vote once again. This time it bowed to the inevitable, but just barely. Even now, when the amendment was certain to pass, there was no rush to get on the bandwagon: thirty senators still voted no. Of the thirteen new men, however, eleven voted for the amendment. The women took no time for rejoicing: they were already busy with the drive for ratification.

Ratification: The Final Step

A constitutional amendment must be approved by legislatures (or special conventions) in three-fourths of the states. The federal system had presented American suffragists with difficult political and legal problems from the beginning and the difficulties were to continue to the very end. The magic number was thirty-six, and eleven ratifications came in the first month. The next five months brought eleven more ratifications. While the proponents of suffrage needed the support of thirty-six states, opponents had to hold only *thirteen* states to block ratification, and the opposition was never more active.

With an eye on the electoral votes already affected by woman suffrage, the national committees of both parties urged speedy ratification. As is usual with state legislators, however, local conditions were more important than the preferences of national leaders. Weary, but by now experienced, local suffrage organizations went to work. Armed with well-researched lists of governors and legislators they began again the process of persuasion. Mrs. Catt travelled where ever she was needed and the Woman's Party deployed its organizers.

By August 1920 thirty-five states had ratified and only one state remained in which ratification was deemed feasible before the presidential election. A special session of the Tennessee legislature was scheduled to begin on August 9 and suffragists and opponents poured into Nashville. It was a wild ten days. The liquor interests, railroad lobby and manufacturers lobby were all active. Opponents of suffrage set up shop on the 8th floor of the Hermitage Hotel and "dispensed Old Bourbon and moonshine whisky with lavish insistence."[16] There was considerable intoxication and on one dismal night, reports circulated that the entire legislature was drunk. In any case by August 13 state senators were sober enough to ratify the amendment by a vote of twenty-five to four.

The contest now swirled around the lower House. There were rumors of deals and bribes and offers of loans on attractive terms. Supporters the suffragists had counted on mysteriously defected, and it was alleged that an attempt was made to kidnap a suffrage member. The vote was so close that it turned on the decision of twenty-four year old Harry Burn, the youngest member of the legislature. In the end he supported suffrage because, so legend has it, his mother urged him to "help Mrs. Catt." The amendment carried by forty-nine to forty-seven.

In the early morning hours of August 26, 1920 the United States secretary of state issued a formal proclamation, and the struggle was over. Seventy-two years had passed since the women at Seneca Falls resolved to "seek their sacred right to the elective franchise." Everywhere in the United States women had the legal right to vote.

Notes

1. Christabel Pankhurst, *Unshackled: The Story of How We Won The Vote* (London: Hutchinson, 1959), p. 83. Such a spirit supplies great energy to a social movement; it pervades the personal documents of the women who did the work in NAWSA and in the Woman's Party. By the time of the first House victory in January 1918 many members of Congress had come to share the sense of a great cause, and some went to extraordinary lengths to insure the success of the amendment on that occasion. The feeling of solidarity in a good cause is powerful.

2. Maud Wood Park, *Front Door Lobby* (Boston: Beacon Press, 1960. Copyright © 1960 by Edna Lamprey Stantial. Reprinted by permission of Beacon Press), p. 19.

3. Park, *Front Door Lobby*, p. 44.

4. Inez Hayes Irwin, *Story of the Woman's Party* (New York: Harcourt—Brace, 1921), p. 334.

5. Carrie Chapman Catt and Nettie R. Shuler, *Woman Suffrage and Politics* (New York: Charles Scribner's Sons, 1923), p. 318. The figure of two million is based on Aileen Kraditor's careful estimates. See *Ideas of the Woman Suffrage Movement* (New York: Columbia University Press, 1965), p. 45.

6. Ethel Smith to Maud Wood Park, October 10, 1917, Maud Wood Park Papers, Schlesinger Library, Cambridge, Massachusetts.

7. Park, *Front Door Lobby*, p. 71.

8. Doris Stevens, *Jailed for Freedom* (New York: Boni and Liveright, 1920), p. 82.

9. Loretta Zimmerman, "Alice Paul and the National Woman's Party" (PH.D. dissertation, Tulane University, 1964), p. 241.

10. Report of the National Congressional Committee, December 1, 1917-January 11, 1918. Maud Wood Park Papers, Schlesinger Library, Cambridge, Massachusetts.

11. Ray Stannard Baker, *Woodrow Wilson: Life and Letters* (New York: Doubleday Page and Co., 1927), vol. VII, p. 460.

12. Memo in Maud Wood Park Papers, Schlesinger Library, Cambridge, Massachusetts. These papers are filled with information concerning the effort to turn the Senate around.

13. U.S., Congress, Senate, Document 284, 65th Cong. 1st sess.

14. These comments were reported in *The Literary Digest* 59 (October 12, 1918). 12-13.

15. P. Orman Ray, "American Government and Politics," *American Political Science Review* 12, no. 1 (Feb. 1910). pp. 80-84.

16. Catt and Shuler, *Woman Suffrage*, p. 442. See also A. Elizabeth Taylor, *The Woman Suffrage Movement in Tennessee* (New York: Bookman Associates, 1957), chapter 7.

Epilogue

In the preceding pages we have tried to illuminate the main points which need to be understood about the long battle for the Nineteenth Amendment:

—the disadvantaged position of women in a society dominated by men;

—the role of male prejudice in perpetuating that disadvantaged position;

—the importance of the ideals of democracy, equality, and natural rights in the American political tradition;

—the enduring tension between those ideals, on the one hand, and a cultural tradition, on the other, which embodied male prejudices and preferences;

—the way the woman suffrage movement related to the broader feminist movement in the United States;

—the characteristics of the leading women actors in the suffrage drama and the roles they played;

—the way the movement developed, including the role of leaders, ideology, recruitment, a mass base and divisions in the movement;

—the peculiar dilemmas and problems faced by an out-group with little political power as it tries to find ways to acquire and exercise political power;

—finally, the political education of suffragists as they learned, often the hard way, about Congress and congressmen, political parties and party leaders, lobbying, campaigning, the techniques of their opponents, methods of organization, and as they fashioned the strategy and tactics that finally brought success.

Was that success worth the effort? The answer depends on the assumptions that are made and the elements that are weighed. Several historians have maintained that suffrage was a "failure." "The ballot," one remarks, "did not materially help women to advance their most urgent causes; even worse, it did not help women to better themselves or improve their status."[1] The line of argument is a familiar one. Women have not succeeded in cleaning up politics, reforming society or ending wars, therefore suffrage is a failure. Women do not even vote as a bloc to support women's issues; clear evidence, presumably, of the uselessness of the vote for women. For such writers, the worth of suffrage is to be measured by the concrete achievements of women using the vote—and standards are to be set high. But, if using the vote wisely is to be made the measure of entitlement to it, men would have had to be disfranchised long ago.

Why did women deserve the vote? Not because they would use it to remake the world or advance their own interests, but because they were entitled to it. If one accepts the central democratic principle, consent of the governed, then women should have the vote and participate in the decisions of the government under which they live. All other arguments are secondary.

To argue that suffrage failed because women have not voted as a bloc is curious, since most political issues do not divide on sex lines. Indeed, in 1916 a writer in the *New York Times*, looking at the effort of the Woman's Party to defeat the Democrats, saw this as grounds for alarm, and charged that "woman suffrage will make in politics a division along sex lines . . . it is an ugly portent." A Woman's Party member reassured him, noting that the existence of a woman's party was the result of *withholding* the vote from women, not of granting it.[2] Since there was no practical possibility of a woman's bloc, its failure to appear is not a reasonable basis for criticism.

Certainly the ballot *has* helped women to improve their status in a number of ways. Since enfranchisement women have been able to move into the political parties and to hold local, state, and national offices. Women are not yet as politically effective as they should be, given their numbers, but the situation has improved considerably since the coming of suffrage.

One must be uninformed to argue that the ballot did not materially help women to advance their most urgent causes. In the past half-century women's organizations have been instrumental in extracting legislation from state and federal legislatures on a wide variety of issues, including some affecting their own status. Can anyone argue seriously that the various equal pay bills or the prohibition of sexual discrimination in the Civil Rights Act of 1964 would have passed if women had not had the vote? Or that affirmative action would now be a policy of the federal government? Or that three presidents and innumerable state governors would have appointed commissions on the status of women? "We soon discovered," wrote an Illinois suffragist in 1920, "that there was no class of people for whom a politician has so tender and respectful a regard as his voting constituents." Enfranchisment by itself is not enough, to be sure, but it provides the foundation on which other efforts can rest.

A second bit of depreciation of the suffrage campaign which surfaces from time to time is the assertion that the effort was probably unnecessary since the ballot would soon have been granted anyway. It is true that women gained the vote in most western nations at about the same time. But it is also true that it was in the democratic societies that women had to work most diligently in their own behalf. It is hard to see how anyone familiar with the history of the suffrage movement in the United States can argue that women were about to be given the vote without a fight. Things happened because, tens, hundreds, and finally millions of women devoted their energies to suffrage. If, a half-century later, woman's suffrage can take on the appearance of historical inevitability it is only because of the work of the Stantons and Anthonys and Catts and their countless coworkers. Several decades from now historians may argue that the women of the 1960s and 1970s need not have agitated themselves so much to oppose various forms of discrimination, bias and prejudice because the situation would have improved without their efforts. The women who worked to bring change will know better.

Finally, it is sometimes said that after the passage of the Nineteenth Amendment women became disillusioned, young women had little feminist ambition, and feminism as a social movement died. The truth is more complicated than that.

We have argued that suffrage became the symbolic focus of feminism, and as a result the woman's movement for a while took on the semblance of a single issue movement. Organization around a single issue has great advantages:

it provides a focus, it eliminates argument about priorities, and permits concentration of effort. Defeats and setbacks become an incentive to try harder.

Single issue movements by their very nature do not survive success. While the suffrage movement was going full speed ahead few people had time to ask, what do we do after we win? Perhaps even those who knew better assumed that somehow attaining the long sought goal would bring in its train fundamental changes in the role and status of women in American life. Victory, then, brought an unforeseen crisis.

Feminism, defined as the fundamental drive of women for autonomy, did not die, nor will it as long as women remain socially, politically, and economically disadvantaged, but the broader social movement we have described lost momentum. Partly this was because one significant group of feminists turned at once to other issues—social welfare, peace, consumer legislation. The League of Women Voters, successor to NAWSA, continued to concern itself with the legal status of women and the plight of women workers, but only as one part of a broad platform.

The National Woman's Party, at the other extreme, concentrated on one thing—the Equal Rights Amendment—but in so doing alienated a great many women who had worked for protective legislation for women workers which they feared would be eliminated by such an amendment. The rivalry which had been productive when both groups wanted the same outcome, now became destructive as women failed to agree on goals and as women in each camp came to think ill of the motives of the other.

The allocation of sex roles and responsibilities in American society did not change substantially in the two decades after suffrage, as William Chafe has persuasively demonstrated in a recent book.[3] While there were an increasing number of women wage earners, they were largely in low-paid, low-status jobs. The number of professional women increased, but largely in "women's fields", such as teaching and social work. The number of working wives increased, but household responsibilities continued to be seen as women's responsibility. There were individual feminists, numbers of whom continued to be sensitive to discrimination in the law and in attitudes, but they had no very large following. Meantime, public opinion polls testified to the pervasiveness of traditional attitudes.

Feminism as a powerful social movement did not emerge again until the 1960s when the publication of Betty Friedan's *Feminine Mystique* energized many educated middle class women, and the Woman's Liberation movement similarly energized many young women. In the past decade the new feminism has permeated almost every sector of the female culture in differing degrees, and the end is not yet in sight.

Why *then*, one might ask, and not fifteen years earlier or fifteen years later? An answer cannot be given with any assurance because the deeper pulses and rhythms of the nation's life are imperfectly understood. Reform seems to come in waves. The struggle for suffrage was given a strong impetus during the Progressive Era, even though women did not win the vote formally until after World War I. The next period in which one might have expected women's issues to be strongly agitated would have been during the Depression and the New Deal, but a cluster of economic issues preempted attention. The Second World War changed women's work roles, but there was not much improvement in their power. After the New Deal the next period of turmoil and reformist agitation was the 1960s. Economic issues were far less important and concerns relating to justice, and the character and quality of American life were foremost. Blacks pressed their demands, young people insisted on being heard, and the woman's movement, stimulated by the Civil Rights movement, suddenly emerged as a major part of the new social consciousness.

It reemerged with a broad basis of concern and hence was in no danger of becoming preoccupied with a single issue. In that sense women were returning to the conception embodied in the Seneca Falls Declaration. After all, only one of the Seneca Falls resolutions dealt with suffrage, and the question of how second-class citizens became first-class citizens could only be answered in part by suffrage.

Women are engaged once more in an energetic and persistent effort to achieve dignity and self-respect, and an opportunity to play a full part in American life. They are not satisfied merely to get along in a man's world; they want to change that world so that it belongs to both sexes. A long road stretches ahead; but a long road has already been travelled.

Notes

1. William L. O'Neill, *Everyone Was Brave: The Rise and Fall of Feminism in American* (Chicago: Quadrangle Books, 1969), p. vii.

2. *New York Times*, July 14, 21 and 22, 1916.

3. William H. Chafe, *The American Woman.* (New York: Oxford University Press, 1972).

Part two

Documents of the Decision

1

Women in Seventeenth-Century England

In an anonymous essay, a seventeenth-century English legal scholar dealt, among other things, with the reasons women were not permitted to vote.

Document†

In this consolidation which we call wedlock is a locking together. It is true, that man and wife are one person; but understand in what manner. When a small brooke or little river incorporateth with Rhodanus, Humber, or the Thames, the poor rivulet looseth her name; it is carried and recarried with the new associate; it beareth no sway; it possesseth nothing during coverture. A woman as soon as she is married, is called *covert*; in Latine *nupta*, that is, "veiled"; as it were, clouded and overshadowed; she hath lost her streame. I may more truly, farre away, say to a married woman, Her new self is her superior; her companion, her master ... Eve, because she had helped to seduce her husband, had inflicted upon her a special bane. See here the reason of that which I touched before,—that women have no voice in Parliament. They make no laws, they consent to none, they abrogate none. All of them are understood either married, or to be married, and their desires are to their husbands. I know no remedy, that some can shift it well enough. The common laws here shaketh hand with divinitye.

†From: *The Lawes Resolutions of Women's Rights; Or, the Lawes Provisions for Women.* (London, 1632).

2

An Early Feminist

An exchange of letters between Abigail Adams and her husband John Adams in the spring of 1776 indicated that not all American women were oblivious to their political deprivation.

Document†

Abigail Adams to John Adams—March 31, 1776 ... —I long to hear that you have declared an independancy—and by the way in the new Code of Laws which I suppose it will be necessary for you to make I desire you would Remember the Ladies, and be more generous and favourable to them than your ancestors. Do not put such unlimited power into the hands of the Husbands. Remember all Men would be tyrants if they could. If perticuliar care and attention is not paid to the Laidies we are determined to foment a Rebelion, and will not hold ourselves bound by any Laws in which we have no voice, or Representation.

That your Sex are Naturally Tyrannical is a Truth so thoroughly established as to admit of no dispute, but such of you as wish to be happy willingly give up the harsh title of Master for the more tender and endearing one of Friend. Why then, not put it out of the power of the vicious and the Lawless to use us with cruelty and indignity with impunity. Men of Sense in all Ages abhor those customs which treat us only as the vassals of your Sex. Regard us then as Beings placed by providence under your protection and in immitation of the Supreem Being make use of that power only for our happiness.

John Adams to Abigail Adams—April 14, 1776 As to your extraordinary Code of Laws, I cannot but laugh. We have been told that our Struggle has loosened the bands of Government every where. That Children and Apprentices were disobedient—that schools and Colledges were grown turbulent—that Indians slighted their Guardians and Negroes grew insolent to their Masters. But your Letter was the first Intimation that another Tribe more numerous and powerfull than all the rest were grown discontended.— This is rather too coarse a Compliment but you are so saucy, I wont blot it out.

Depend upon it, We know better than to repeal our Masculine systems. Altho they are in full Force, you know they are little more than Theory. We dare not exert our Power in its full Latitude. We are obliged to go fair, and softly, and in Practice you know We are the subjects. We have only the Name

†From: L.H. Butterfield, ed. *Adams Family Correspondence* (Cambridge: The Belknap Press of Harvard University Press, 1963), vol. I, pp. 370, 382, 402. Copyright 1963 by The Massachusetts Historical Society.

of Masters, and rather than give up this, which would compleatly subject Us to the Despotism of the Peticoat, I hope General Washington, and all our brave Heroes would fight. I am sure every good Politician would plot, as long as he would against Despotism, Empire, Monarchy, Aristocracy, Oligarchy, or Ochlocracy—A fine Story indeed. I begin to think the Ministry as deep as they are wicked. After stirring up Tories, Landjobbers, Trimmers, Bigots, Canadians, Indians, Negroes, Hanoverians, Hessians, Russians, Irish Roman Catholicks, Scotch Renegadoes, at last they have stimulated the [women] to demand new Priviledges and threaten to rebell.

Abigail Adams to John Adams—May 7, 1776 I can not say that I think you very generous to the Ladies, for whilst you are proclaming peace and good will to Men, Emancipating all Nations, you insist upon retaining an absolute power over Wives. But you must remember that Arbitary power is like most other things which are very hard, very liable to be broken—and notwithstanding all your wise Laws and Maxims we have it in our power not only to free ourselves but to subdue our Masters, and without voilence throw both your natural and legal authority at our feet—

. . .

3

"Declaration of Sentiments"

The Seneca Falls Declaration, read carefully, tells a good deal about the particular grievances women felt.

Document†

Declaration of Sentiments

When, in the course of human events, it becomes necessary for one portion of the family of man to assume among the people of the earth a position different from that which they have hitherto occupied, but one to which the laws of nature and of nature's God entitle them, a decent respect to the opinions of mankind requires that they should declare the causes that impel them to such a course.

We hold these truths to be self-evident: that all men and women are created equal; that they are endowed by their Creator with certain inalienable rights; that among these are life, liberty, and the pursuit of happiness; that to secure these rights governments are instituted, deriving their just powers from the consent of the governed. Whenever any form of government becomes destructive of these ends, it is the right of those who suffer from it to refuse allegiance to it, and to insist upon the institution of a new government, laying its foundation on such principles, and organizing its powers in such form, as to them shall seem most likely to effect their safety and happiness. Prudence, indeed, will dictate that governments long established should not be changed for light and transient causes; and accordingly all experience hath shown that mankind are more disposed to suffer, while evils are sufferable, than to right themselves by abolishing the forms to which they were accustomed. But when a long train of abuses and usurpations, pursuing invariably the same object, evinces a design to reduce them under absolute despotism, it is their duty to throw off such government, and to provide new guards for their future security. Such has been the patient sufferance of the women under this government, and such is now the necessity which constrains them to demand the equal station to which they are entitled.

The history of mankind is a history of repeated injuries and usurpations on the part of man toward woman, having in direct object the establishment of an absolute tyranny over her. To prove this, let facts be submitted to a candid world.

†From: Susan B. Anthony et al., *History of Woman Suffrage* (Rochester: Susan B. Anthony, 1887), vol. I, pp. 70-71.

He has never permitted her to exercise her inalienable right to the elective franchise.

He has compelled her to submit to laws, in the formation of which she had no voice.

He has withheld from her rights which are given to the most ignorant and degraded men—both natives and foreigners.

Having deprived her of this first right of a citizen, the elective franchise, thereby leaving her without representation in the halls of legislation, he has oppressed her on all sides.

He has made her, if married, in the eye of the law, civilly dead.

He has taken from her all right in property, even to the wages she earns.

He has made her, morally, an irresponsible being, as she can commit many crimes with impunity, provided they be done in the presence of her husband. In the covenant of marriage, she is compelled to promise obedience to her husband, he becoming, to all intents and purposes, her master—the law giving him power to deprive her of her liberty, and to administer chastisement.

He has so framed the laws of divorce, as to what shall be the proper causes, and in case of separation, to whom the guardianship of the children shall be given, as to be wholly regardless of the happiness of women—the law, in all cases, going upon the false supposition of the supremacy of man, and giving all power into his hands.

After depriving her of all rights as a married woman, if single, and the owner of property, he has taxed her to support a government which recognizes her only when her property can be made profitable to it.

He has monopolized nearly all the profitable employments, and from those she is permitted to follow, she receives but a scanty remuneration. He closes against her all the avenues to wealth and distinction which he considers most honorable to himself. As a teacher of theology, medicine, or law, she is not known.

He has denied her the facilities for obtaining a thorough education, all colleges being closed against her.

He allows her in Church, as well as State, but a subordinate position, clamining Apostolic authority for her exclusion from the ministry, and, with some exceptions, from any public participation in the affairs of the Church.

He has created a false public sentiment by giving to the world a different code of morals for men and women, by which moral delinquencies which exclude women from society, are not only tolerated, but deemed of little account in man.

He has usurped the prerogative of Jehovah himself, claiming it as his right to assign for her a sphere of action, when that belongs to her conscience and to her God.

He has endeavored, in every way that he could, to destroy her confidence in her own powers, to lessen her self-respect, and to make her willing to lead a dependent and abject life.

Now, in view of this entire disfranchisement of one-half the people of this country, their social and religious degradation—in view of the unjust laws above mentioned, and because women do feel themselves aggrieved, oppressed, and fraudulently deprived of their most sacred rights, we insist that they have immediate admission to all the rights and privileges which belong to them as citizens of the United States.

In entering upon the great work before us, we anticipate no small amount of misconception, misrepresentation, and ridicule; but we shall use every instrumentality within our power to effect our object. We shall employ agents, circulate tracts, petition the State and National legislatures, and endeavor to enlist the pulpit and the press in our behalf. We hope this Convention will be followed by a series of Conventions embracing every part of the country.

Resolutions: Whereas, The great precept of nature is conceded to be, that "man shall pursue his own true and substantial happiness." Blackstone in his Commentaries remarks, that this law of Nature being coeval with mankind, and dictated by God himself, is of course superior in obligation to any other. It is binding over all the globe, in all countries and at all times; no human laws are of any validity if contrary to this, and such of them as are valid, derive all their force, and all their validity, and all their authority, mediately and immediately, from this original; therefore,

Resolved, That such laws as conflict, in any way, with the true and substantial happiness of woman, are contrary to the great precept of nature and of no validity, for this is "superior in obligation to any other."

Resolved, That all laws which prevent woman from occupying such a station in society as her conscience shall dictate, or which place her in a position inferior to that of man, are contrary to the great precept of nature, and therefore of no force or authority.

Resolved, That woman is man's equal—was intended to be so by the Creator, and the highest good of the race demands that she should be recognized as such.

Resolved, That the women of this country ought to be enlightened in regard to the laws under which they live, that they may no longer publish their degradation by declaring themselves satisfied with their present position, nor their ignorance, by asserting that they have all the rights they want.

Resolved, That inasmuch as man, while claiming for himself intellectual superiority, does accord to woman moral superiority, it is pre-eminently his duty to encourage her to speak and teach, as she has an opportunity, in all religious assemblies.

Resolved, That the same amount of virtue, delicacy, and refinement of behavior that is required of woman in the social state, should also be required of man, and the same transgressions should be visited with equal severity on both man and woman.

Resolved, That the objection of indelicacy and impropriety, which is so often brought against woman when she addresses a public audience, comes with a very ill-grace from those who encourage, by their attendance, her appearance on the stage, in the concert, or in feats of the circus.

Resolved, That woman has too long rested satisfied in the circumscribed limits which corrupt customs and a perverted application of the Scriptures have marked out for her, and that it is time she should move in the enlarged sphere which her great Creator has assigned her.

Resolved, That it is the duty of the women of this country to secure to themselves their sacred right to the elective franchise.

Resolved, That the equality of human rights results necessarily from the fact of the identity of the race in capabilities and responsibilities.

Resolved, therefore, That, being invested by the Creator with the same capabilities, and the same consciousness of responsibility for their exercise, it is demonstrably the right and duty of woman, equally with man, to promote every righteous cause by every righteous means; and especially in regard to the great subjects of morals and religion, it is self-evidently her right to participate with her brother in teaching them, both in private and in public, by writing and by speaking, by any instrumentalities proper to be used, and in any assemblies proper to be held; and this being a self-evident truth growing out of the divinely implanted principles of human nature, any custom or authority adverse to it, whether modern or wearing the hoary sanction of antiquity, is to be regarded as a self-evident falsehood, and at war with mankind.

Resolved, That the speedy success of our cause depends upon the zealous and untiring efforts of both men and women, for the overthrow of the monopoly of the pulpit, and for the securing to woman an equal participation with men in the various trades, professions, and commerce.

4-a

Elizabeth Cady Stanton on the Politics of Woman Suffrage

At the first woman suffrage convention held in Washington, Mrs. Stanton discussed the rationale for a woman suffrage amendment, and went on to analyze the politics of getting such an amendment. The rivalry between the parties she hoped to stir up was a long time coming: this speech would have been à propos in 1918, when the Democrats were about to give over control of the Congress to the Republicans. The excerpts here not only provide the substance of Stanton's thinking, but are a good example of her vigorous style.

Document†

Those who represent what is called "the Woman's Rights Movement," have argued their right to political equality from every standpoint of justice, religion, and logic, for the last twenty years. They have quoted the Constitution, the Declaration of Independence, the Bible, the opinions of great men and women in all ages; they have plead the theory of our government; suffrage a natural, inalienable right; shown from the lessons of history, that one class can not legislate for another; that disfranchised classes must ever be neglected and degraded; and that all privileges are but mockery to the citizen, until he has a voice in the making and administering of law. Such arguments have been made over and over in conventions and before the legislatures of the several States. Judges, lawyers, priests, and politicians have said again and again, that our logic was unanswerable, and although much nonsense has emanated from the male tongue and pen on this subject, no man has yet made a fair, argument on the other side. Knowing that we hold the Gibraltar rock of reason on this question, they resort to ridicule and petty objections. Compelled to follow our assailants, wherever they go, and fight them with their own weapons; when cornered with wit and sarcasm, some cry out, you have no logic on your platform, forgetting that we have no use for logic until they give us logicians at whom to hurl it, and if, for the pure love of it, we now and then rehearse the logic that is like a, b, c, to all of us, others cry out—the same old speeches we have heard these twenty years. It would be

†From: Susan B. Anthony et al., *History of Woman Suffrage* (Rochester: Susan B. Anthony, 1869), vol. II, pp. 348-55.

safe to say a hundred years, for they are the same our fathers used when battling old King George and the British Parliament for their right to representation, and a voice in the laws by which they were governed. There are no new arguments to be made on human rights, our work to-day is to apply to ourselves those so familiar to all; to teach man that woman is not an anomalous being, outside all laws and constitutions, but one whose rights are to be established by the same process of reason as that by which he demands his own.

When our Fathers made out their famous bill of impeachment against England, they specified eighteen grievances. When the women of this country surveyed the situation in their first convention, they found they had precisely that number, and quite similar in character; and reading over the old revolutionary arguments of Jefferson, Patrick Henry, Otis, and Adams, they found they applied remarkably well to their case. The same arguments made in this country for extending suffrage from time to time, to white men, native born citizens, without property and education, and to foreigners; the same used by John Bright in England, to extend it to a million new voters, and the same used by the great Republican party to enfranchise a million black men in the South, all these arguments we have to-day to offer for woman, and one, in addition, stronger than all besides, the difference in man and woman. Because man and woman are the complement of one another, we need woman's thought in national affairs to make a safe and stable government.

The Republican party to-day congratulates itself on having carried the Fifteenth Amendment of the Constitution, thus securing "manhood suffrage" and establishing an aristocracy of sex on this continent. As several bills to secure Woman's Suffrage in the District and the Territories have been already presented in both houses of Congress, and as by Mr. Julian's bill, the question of so amending the Constitution as to extend suffrage to all the women of the country has been presented to the nation for consideration, it is not only the right but the duty of every thoughtful woman to express her opinion on a Sixteenth Amendment. While I hail the late discussions in Congress and the various bills presented as so many signs of progress, I am especially gratified with those of Messrs. Julian and Pomeroy, which forbid any State to deny the right of suffrage to any of its citizens on account of sex or color.

This fundamental principle of our government—the equality of all the citizens of the republic—should be incorporated in the Federal Constitution, there to remain forever. To leave this question to the States and partial acts of Congress, is to defer indefinitely its settlement, for what is done by this Congress may be repealed by the next; and politics in the several States differ so widely, that no harmonious action on any question can ever be secured, except as a strict party measure. Hence, we appeal to the party now in power, everywhere, to end this protracted debate on suffrage, and declare it the inalienable right of every citizen who is amenable to the laws of the land, who pays taxes and the penalty of crime. We have a splendid theory of a genuine republic, why not realize it and make our government homogeneous, from Maine to California. The Republican party has the power to do this, and now is its only opportunity. Woman's Suffrage, in 1872, may be as good a card for the Republicans as Gen. Grant was in the last election. It is said that the Republican party made him President, not because they thought him the most desirable man in the nation for that office, but they were afraid the Democrats would take him if they did not. We would suggest, there may be the same danger of Democrats taking up Woman Suffrage if they do not. God, in his providence, may have purified that party in the furnace of affliction. They have had the opportunity, safe from the turmoil of political life and the temptations of office, to study and apply the divine principles of justice and equality to life; for minorities are always in a position to carry principles to their logical results, while majorities are governed only by votes. You see my faith in Democrats is based on sound philosophy. In the next Congress, the Democratic party will gain thirty-four new members, hence the Republicans have had their last chance to do justice to woman. It will be no enviable record for the Fortieth Congress that in the darkest days of the republic it placed our free institutions in the care and keeping of every type of manhood, ignoring womanhood, all the elevating and purifying influences of the most virtuous and humane half of the American people. . . .

I urge a speedy adoption of a Sixteenth Amendment for the following reasons:

1. A government, based on the principle of caste and class, can not stand. The aristocratic idea, in any form, is opposed to the genius of our free institutions, to our own declaration of rights, and to the civilization of the age. All artificial distinctions, whether of family, blood, wealth, color, or sex, are equally oppressive to the subject classes, and equally destructive to national life and prosperity. Governments based on every form of aristocracy, on every degree and variety of inequality, have been tried in despotisms, monarchies, and republics, and all alike have perished. . . . Thus far, all nations have been built on caste and failed. Why, in this hour of reconstruction, with the experience of generations before us, make another experiment in the same direction? If serfdom, peasantry, and slavery have shattered kingdoms, deluged continents with blood, scattered republics like dust before the wind, and rent our own Union asunder, what kind of a government, think you, American statesmen, you can build, with the mothers of the race crouching at your feet, while iron-heeled peasants, serfs, and slaves, exalted by your hands, tread our inalienable rights into the dust? While all men, everywhere, are rejoicing in new-found liberties, shall woman alone be denied the rights, privileges, and immunities of citizenship? While in England men are coming up from the coal mines of Cornwall, from the factories of Birmingham and Manchester, demanding the suffrage; while in frigid Russia the 22,000,000 newly-emancipated serfs are already claiming a voice in the government; while here, in our own land, slaves, but just rejoicing in the proclamation of emancipation, ignorant alike of its power and significance, have the ballot unasked, unsought, already laid at their feet—think you the daughters of Adams, Jefferson, and Patrick Henry, in whose veins flows the blood of two Revolutions, will forever linger round the

camp-fires of an old barbarism, with no longings to join this grand army of freedom in its onward march to roll back the golden gates of a higher and better civilization? Of all kinds of aristocracy, that of sex is the most odious and unnatural; invading, as it does, our homes, desecrating our family altars, dividing those whom God has joined together, exalting the son above the mother who bore him, and subjugating, everywhere, moral power to brute force. Such a government would not be worth the blood and treasure so freely poured out in its long struggles for freedom. . . .

2. I urge a Sixteenth Amendment, because "manhood suffrage" or a man's government, is civil, religious, and social disorganization. The male element is a destructive force, stern, selfish, aggrandizing, loving war, violence, conquest, acquisition, breeding in the material and moral world alike discord, disorder, disease, and death. See what a record of blood and cruelty the pages of history reveal! Through what slavery, slaughter, and sacrifice, through what inquisitions and imprisonments, pains and persecutions, black codes and gloomy creeds, the soul of humanity has struggled for the centuries, while mercy has veiled her face and all hearts have been dead alike to love and hope! The male element has held high carnival thus far, it has fairly run riot from the beginning, overpowering the feminine element everywhere, crushing out all the diviner qualities in human nature, until we know but little of true manhood and womanhood, of the latter comparatively nothing, for it has scarce been recognized as a power until within the last century. Society is but the reflection of man himself, untempered by woman's thought, the hard iron rule we feel alike in the church, the state, and the home. No one need wonder at the disorganization, at the fragmentary condition of everything, when we remember that man, who represents but half a complete being, with but half an idea on every subject, has undertaken the absolute control of all sublunary matters.

People object to the demands of those whom they choose to call the strong-minded, because they say, "the right of suffrage will make the women masculine." That is just the difficulty in which we are involved to-day. Though disfranchised we have few women in the best sense, we have simply so many reflections, varieties, and dilutions of the masculine gender. The strong, natural characteristics of womanhood are repressed and ignored in dependence, for so long as man feeds woman she will try to please the giver and adapt herself to his condition. To keep a foothold in society woman must be as near like man as possible, reflect his ideas, opinions, virtues, motives, prejudices, and vices. She must respect his statutes, though they strip her of every inalienable right, and conflict with that higher law written by the finger of God on her own soul. She must believe his theology, though it pave the highways of hell with the skulls of new-born infants, and make God a monster of vengeance and hypocrisy. She must look at everything from its dollar and cent point of view, or she is a mere romancer. She must accept things as they are and make the best of them. To mourn over the miseries of others, the poverty of the poor, their hardships in jails, prisons, asylums, the horrors of war, cruelty, and brutality in every form, all this would be mere sentimentalizing. To protest against the intrigue, bribery, and corruption of public life, to desire that her sons might follow some business that did not involve lying, cheating, and a hard, grinding selfishness, would be arrant nonsense. In this way man has been moulding woman to his ideas by direct and positive influences, while she, if not a negation, has used indirect means to control him, and in most cases developed the very characteristics both in him and herself that needed repression. And now man himself stands appalled at the results of his own excesses, and mourns in bitterness that falsehood, selfishness and violence are the law of life. The need of this hour is not territory, gold mines, railroads, or specie payments, but a new evangel of womanhood, to exalt purity, virtue, morality, true religion, to lift man up into the higher realms of thought and action.

We ask woman's enfranchisement, as the first step toward the recognition of that essential element in government that can only secure the health, strength, and prosperity of the nation. Whatever is done to lift woman to her true position will help to usher in a new day of peace and perfection for the race. In speaking of the masculine element, I do not wish to be understood to say that all men are hard, selfish, and brutal, for many of the most beautiful spirits the world has known have been clothed with manhood; but I refer to those characteristics, though often marked in woman, that distinguish what is called the stronger sex. For example, the love of acquisition and conquest, the very pioneers of civilization, when expended on the earth, the sea, the elements, the riches and forces of Nature, are powers of destruction when used to subjugate one man to another or to sacrifice nations to ambition. Here that great conservator of woman's love, if permitted to assert itself, as it naturally would in freedom against oppression, violence, and war, would hold all these destructive forces in check, for woman knows the cost of life better than man does, and not with her consent would one drop of blood ever be shed, one life sacrificed in vain. With violence and disturbance in the natural world, we see a constant effort to maintain an equilibrium of forces. Nature, like a loving mother, is ever trying to keep land and sea, mountain and valley, each in its place, to hush the angry winds and waves, balance the extremes of heat and cold, of rain and drought, that peace, harmony, and beauty may reign supreme. There is a striking analogy between matter and mind, and the present disorganization of society warns us, that in the dethronement of woman we have let loose the elements of violence and ruin that she only has the power to curb. If the civilization of the age calls for an extension of the suffrage, surely a government of the most virtuous, educated men and women would better represent the whole, and protect the interests of all than could the representation of either sex alone. But government gains no new element of strength in admitting all men to the ballot-box, for we have too much of the man-power there already. We see this in every department of legislation, and it is a common remark, that unless some new virtue is infused into our public life the nation is doomed to destruction. Will the foreign element, the dregs of China, Germany, England, Ireland, and Africa supply this needed force, or the nobler types of American womanhood who have taught our presidents, senators, and congressmen the rudiments of all they know?

3. I urge a Sixteenth Amendment because, when "manhood suffrage" is established from Maine to California, woman has reached the lowest depths of political degradation. So long as there is a disfranchised class in this country, and that class its women, a man's government is worse than a white man's government with suffrage limited by property and educational qualifications, because in proportion as you multiply the rulers, the condition of the politically ostracised is more hopeless and degraded. John Stuart Mill, in his work on "Liberty," shows that the condition of one disfranchised man in a nation is worse than when the whole nation is under one man, because in the latter case, if the one man is despotic, the nation can easily throw him off, but what can one man do with a nation of tyrants over him? If American women find it hard to bear the oppressions of their own Saxon fathers, the best orders of manhood, what may they not be called to endure when all the lower orders of foreigners now crowding our shores legislate for them and their daughters. Think of Patrick and Sambo and Hans and Yung Tung, who do not know the difference between a monarchy and a republic, who can not read the Declaration of Independence or Webster's spelling-book, making laws for Lucretia Mott, Ernestine L. Rose, and Anna E. Dickinson. Think of jurors and jailors drawn from these ranks to watch and try young girls for the crime of infanticide, to decide the moral code by which the mothers of this Republic shall be governed? This manhood suffrage is an appalling question, and it would be well for thinking women, who seem to consider it so magnanimous to hold their own claims in abeyance until all men are crowned with citizenship, to remember that the most ignorant men are ever the most hostile to the equality of women, as they have known them only in slavery and degradation.

Go to our courts of justice, our jails and prisons; go into the world of work; into the trades and professions; into the temples of science and learning, and see what is meted out everywhere to women—to those who have no advocates in our courts, no representatives in the councils of the nation. Shall we prolong and perpetuate such injustice, and by increasing this power risk worse oppressions for ourselves and daughters? It is an open, deliberate insult to American womanhood to be cast down under the iron-heeled peasantry of the Old World and the slaves of the New, as we shall be in the practical working of the Fifteenth Amendment, and the only atonement the Republican party can make is now to complete its work, by enfranchising the women of the nation. I have not forgotten their action four years ago, when Article XIV., Sec. 2, was amended* by invidiously introducing the word "male" into the Federal Constitution, where it had never been before, thus

---

*The amendment as proposed by the Hon. Thaddeus Stevens, of Pennsylvania, extended the right of suffrage to "all citizens," which included both white and black women. At the bare thought of such an impending calamity, the more timid Republicans were filled with alarm, and the word "male" promptly inserted.

counting out of the basis of representation all men not permitted to vote, thereby making it the interest of every State to enfranchise its male citizens, and virtually declaring it no crime to disfranchise its women. As political sagacity moved our rulers thus to guard the interests of the negro for party purposes, common justice might have compelled them to show like respect for their own mothers, by counting woman too out of the basis of representation, that she might no longer swell the numbers to legislate adversely to her interests. And this desecration of the last will and testament of the fathers, this retrogressive legislation for woman, was in the face of the earnest protests of thousands of the best educated, most refined and cultivated women of the North.

Now, when the attention of the whole world is turned to this question of suffrage, and women themselves are throwing off the lethargy of ages, and in England, France, Germany, Switzerland, and Russia are holding their conventions, and their rulers are everywhere giving them a respectful hearing, shall American statesmen, claiming to be liberal, so amend their constitutions as to make their wives and mothers the political inferiors of unlettered and unwashed ditch-diggers, boot-blacks, butchers, and barbers, fresh from the slave plantations of the South, and the effete civilizations of the Old World? While poets and philosophers, statesmen and men of science are all alike pointing to woman as the new hope for the redemption of the race, shall the freest Government on the earth be the first to establish an aristocracy based on sex alone? to exalt ignorance above education, vice above virtue, brutality and barbarism above refinement and religion? Not since God first called light out of darkness and order out of chaos, was there ever made so base a proposition as "manhood suffrage" in this American Republic, after all the discussions we have had on human rights in the last century. On all the blackest pages of history there is no record of an act like this, in any nation, where native born citizens, having the same religion, speaking the same language, equal to their rulers in wealth, family, and education, have been politically ostracised by their own countrymen, outlawed with savages, and subjected to the government of outside barbarians. Remember the Fifteenth Amendment takes in a larger population than the 2,000,000 black men on the Southern plantation. It takes in all the foreigners daily landing in our eastern cities, the Chinese crowding our western shores, the inhabitants of Alaska, and all those western isles that will soon be ours. American statesmen may flatter themselves that by superior intelligence and political sagacity the higher orders of men will always govern, but when the ignorant foreign vote already holds the balance of power in all the large cities by sheer force of numbers, it is simply a question of impulse or passion, bribery or fraud, how our elections will be carried. When the highest offices in the gift of the people are bought and sold in Wall Street, it is a mere chance who will be our rulers. Whither is a nation tending when brains count for less than bullion, and clowns make laws for queens? It is a startling assertion, but nevertheless true, that in none of the nations of modern Europe are the higher classes of women politically so degraded as are the women of this Republic to-day. In the Old

World, where the government is the aristocracy, where it is considered a mark of nobility to share its offices and powers, women of rank have certain hereditary rights which raise them above a majority of the men, certain honors and privileges not granted to serfs and peasants. There women are queens, hold subordinate offices, and vote on many questions. In our Southern States even, before the war, women were not degraded below the working population. They were not humiliated in seeing their coachmen, gardeners, and waiters go to the polls to legislate for them, but here, in this boasted Northern civilization, women of wealth and education, who pay taxes and obey the laws, who in morals and intellect are the peers of their proudest rulers, are thrust outside the pale of political consideration with minors, paupers, lunatics, traitors, idiots, with those guilty of bribery, larceny, and infamous crimes.

Would those gentlemen who are on all sides telling the women of the nation not to press their claims until the negro is safe beyond peradventure, be willing themselves to stand aside and trust all their interests to hands like these? The educated women of this nation feel as much interest in republican institutions, the preservation of the country, the good of the race, their own elevation and success, as any man possibly can, and we have the same distrust in man's power to legislate for us, that he has in woman's power to legislate wisely for herself.

4. I would press a Sixteenth Amendment, because the history of American statesmanship does not inspire me with confidence in man's capacity to govern the nation alone, with justice and mercy. I have come to this conclusion, not only from my own observation, but from what our rulers say of themselves. Honorable Senators have risen in their places again and again, and told the people of the wastefulness and corruption of the present administration. Others have set forth, with equal clearness, the ignorance of our rulers on the question of finance. . . . .

4-b

The Woman Suffrage Amendment is Introduced

On May 28, 1874 the Senate was debating the formation of the Territory of Pembina (later North Dakota). Senator A.A. Sargent of California, a good friend of Elizabeth Cady Stanton and strong suffragist, introduced an amendment to provide that the legislature of the territory should not abridge the right to vote or hold office on grounds of sex, race, color or previous condition of servitude. In introducing the amendment Sargent himself developed the argument that under the Fourteenth and Fifteenth Amendments women should be permitted to vote. His opponents offered some of the prevalent antisuffrage arguments, especially that woman suffrage was a contradiction of God's will. The debate filled thirteen pages of the Congressional Record. A few excerpts provide the argument and flavor. Senators then, as now, were not given to brevity. The senators speaking in addition to Sargent were William M. Stewart of Nevada, Oliver P. Morton of Indiana and Thomas F. Bayard of Delaware.

Document†

Provided, That the Legislative Assembly shall not, at any time, abridge the right of suffrage, or to hold office, on account of sex, race, color, or previous condition of servitude of any resident of the Territory.

Mr. SARGENT. In the same connection I move in the first line of section 5 to strike out the word "male," so as to read "every inhabitant of the United States."

The PRESIDENT *pro tempore.* The question is on the amendment of the Senator from California.

Mr. SARGENT. At the time when the last national convention of the republican party assembled in Philadelphia which nominated the present President of the United States for his second term, there was assembled a body of able, respectable ladies of the United States, who urged upon that convention a consideration of the subject involved in the amendment which I propose; and as a concession to the demand made by those persons a plank was inserted in the platform whereby it was declared that the republican party would treat with consideration the claims of women to be admitted to additional rights. . . .

†From: U.S., Congress, Senate, *Congressional Record,* 43rd Cong., 1st sess., pp. 4331-44.

I believe, Mr. President, that the amendment which I offer to this bill is justified by the organic law of the United States, and in fact required by that law. Before the adoption of the fourteenth and fifteenth articles of amendment to the Constitution of the United States women were hedged out of the ballot-box by the use of the word "male." Since that time another rule has been prescribed by the organic law, and it is made the right of all citizens of the United States to approach the ballot-box and exercise this highest privilege of a citizen. By the fourteenth article of amendment it is provided that "all persons born or naturalized in the United States, and subject to the jurisdiction thereof, are citizens of the United States and of the State wherein they reside." This most important declaration is now the organic law of the United States. It does not say "all males born or naturalized in the United States," but "all persons," and it cannot be contended successfully that a woman is not a person, and not a person within the meaning of this clause of the Constitution.

This being the status of all individuals, male and female, they being citizens of the United States, it is provided that "no State shall make or enforce any law which shall abridge the privileges or immunities of citizens of the United States; nor shall any State deprive any person of life, liberty, or property, without due process of law." Of course if any State is prohibited from doing this, any Territory should be prohibited from doing it, because no Territory can constitutionally do that which a State itself cannot do.

Then, if women are citizens of the United States and there is no right to abridge the privileges and immunities of citizens of the United States, as proclaimed by the supreme law of the land, what are these privileges and immunities? [Richard] Grant White, in his able work on Words and Their Uses, defines, on page 100, the privileges and immunities of citizens, and among them gives the right to vote and the right to hold office. Webster gives the same definition of the word "citizen" and so does Worcester, and Bouvier's Law Dictionary speaks expressly of these rights of citizens of the United States to vote, and hold office; and there is little adverse authority to these definitions. . . .

The considerations which I have urged address themselves not merely to republicans, they address themselves with great force to my democratic friends who are such sticklers for the Constitution. Although that is true, nevertheless the republican party has pledged itself especially to a respectful consideration of these demands in its last national platform, and it has control of both Houses of Congress and of the executive department.

Passing from that consideration, we have all persons born or naturalized in the United States declared by the Constitution to be citizens; and we have the meaning of the word "citizen" given by our courts, by our lexicographers, by our law commentators; we have further their "privileges and immunities" settled by all these authorities to include the right to vote and the right to hold office.

In consonance with this organic law, the policy of which is not open to discussion because it has been adopted according to all the legal forms by the people of the United States, I offer this amendment. Were this the time and place, and were not the discussion foreclosed by the considerations which I have already advanced, I might speak at some length upon the advantages which there would be in the admission of women to the suffrage. I might point with some pride to the experiment which has been made in Wyoming where women hold office, where they vote, where they have the most orderly society of any of the Territories, where the experiment is approved by the Executive officers of the United States by their courts, by their press, and by the people generally; and if it operates so well in Wyoming, where it has rescued that Territory from a state of comparative lawlessness to one of the most orderly in the Union, I ask why it might not operate equally well in the Territory of Pembina or any other Territory? I hope the time is not far distant when some of the older States of the Union like New York or Massachusetts or Ohio may give this experiment a fuller chance. But so far as it has gone, the experiment has been entirely in favor of legislation of this character, of admitting women to the ballot-box. And I do not believe that in putting these higher responsibilities upon women we degrade their character, that we subject them to uncongenial pursuits, that we injure their moral tone, that we tarnish their delicacy, that we in any way make them less noble and admirable as women, as wives, and mothers. I believe that by realizing the intention of the Constitution, which uses words that are so fully explained by our courts and by our writers upon the uses of words, we simply open a wider avenue to women for usefulness to themselves and to society. I think we give them an opportunity, instead of traveling the few and confined roads that are open to them now, to engage more generally in the business of life under some guarantee of their success. I believe that, instead of driving them to irregular efforts like those which they recently have made in many of the States to overthrow liquor selling and consumption and its desolation of their homes, it will give them an opportunity through the ballot-box to protect their families, to break up the nefarious traffic, and purify society. As it is now, their energies in this direction are repressed, and sometimes in order to have force are compelled to be exercised even in opposition to law. I would give them an opportunity to exercise them under the forms of law, and I would enforce the law by the accession of this pure element. I do not think that they would be corrupted by it, but rather that society and politics and your laws would be purified by admitting them to the ballot-box and giving them this opportunity. . . .

Mr. STEWART. If this region is to be created into a Territory, I think it eminently proper that this amendment should be adopted. The question of female suffrage is a question that is being seriously considered by a large portion of the people of the United States. We may think lightly of it here; we may think it never will be accomplished; but there are a great many earnest people who believe if females had the ballot they could better protect themselves, be more independent, and occupy useful positions in life which are now denied to them. Whether they be correct or not, it is not necessary for us to determine in passing upon this amendment. Here is a new Territory to be created and it is a good opportunity to try this experiment. If it works badly, when the Territory becomes a State there is nobody committed. It is not an amendment of the organic law of the nation. This is a bill simply providing for the organization of a Territory and for a preliminary government, and I should like for one to see this experiment tried up in the region near Minnesota where this new government is to be inaugurated. If it works well, it may spread elsewhere. It certainly can do no harm in that country. There are very few people there.

It is suggested by my friend on my right [Mr. Conkling] that it cannot spread unless it is catching. [Laughter.] If it works well, if it succeeds in protecting females in their rights and enabling them to assert their rights elsewhere and obtain such employment as is suitable to them, I hope it will become catching and spread all over the country, if that is the light in which it is to be treated. I am in earnest about this matter. I think this new Territory is the place to try the experiment right here. If it works badly, we can see it and no great harm will be done. If it works well, the example will be a good one and will be imitated.

Mr. MORTON. I desire simply to state my views upon this amendment, views long entertained. I am in favor of the amendment upon what I regard as the fundamental principles of our Government, upon the theory upon which we have based our Government from the beginning. The Declaration of Independence says:

> We hold these truths to be self-evident, that all men are created equal; that they are endowed by their Creator with certain unalienable rights; that among these are life, liberty, and the pursuit of happiness.

The word "men" in that connection does not mean males, but it means the human family; that all human beings are created equal. This will hardly be denied. I remember it was formerly contended that the Declaration of Independence in this clause did not include black people. It was argued learnedly and frequently, in this Chamber and out of it, that the history surrounding the adoption of that declaration showed that white men only were intended. But that was not the general judgment of the people of this country. It was held to embrace all colors and all races. It embraces both sexes; not simply males, but females. All human beings are created equal. That is the foundation principle of our Government. It then goes on to say:

> That to secure these rights, governments are instituted among men, deriving their just powers from the consent of the governed; that, whenever any form of government becomes destructive of these ends, it is the right of the people to alter or to abolish it, and to institute a new government, laying its foundation on such principles, and organizing its powers in such form, as to them shall seem most likely to effect their safety and happiness.

If these rights are fundamental, if they belong to all human beings as such, if they are God-given rights, then all persons having these God-given rights have a right to use the means for their preservation. The means is government: "To secure these rights, governments are instituted among men, deriving their just powers from the consent of the governed."

I ask you whether the women of this country have ever given their consent to this Government? Have they the means of giving their consent to it? The colored men had not given their consent to it. Why? Because they had not the right to vote. There is but one way that the consent to government can be given, and that is by a right to a voice in that government, and that is the right to vote. . . .

What was the old theory of the common law? It was that the father represented the interests of his daughter, the husband of his wife, and the son of his mother. They were deprived of all legal rights in a state of marriage, because it was said that they were taken care of by those who stood to them in these relations; but they never were taken care of. The husband never took care of the rights of his wife at common law; the father never took care of the rights of his daughter; the son never took care of the rights of his mother. The husband at common law was a tyrant and a despot. Why, sir, he absorbed the legal existence of his wife at common law; she could not make a contract except as his agent. Her legal existence was destroyed, and the very moment the marriage was consummated he became the absolute owner of all her personal property. What was the theory of it? The old theory of the common law, as given in elementary writers, was that if the wife was allowed to own property separate from her husband it would make a distinct interest; it would break up and destroy the harmony of the marriage relation; the marriage relation must be a unit; there must be but one interest; and therefore the legal existence of the wife must be merged into that of the husband. I believe a writer as late as Blackstone laid it down that it would not do to permit the wife to hold any property in severalty from her husband, becaude it would give to her an interest apart from his.

We have got over that. It took us one hundred and fifty years to get past that, and from year to year in this country, especially in the last twenty-five years, we have added to the rights of the wife in regard to property and in many other respects. We now give to her a legal status in this country that she has not in England or in any European country. She has now a legal status that she had not twenty-five years ago, and progress is still going on in that direction. While it was argued by old law-writers and old law-makers that to allow women to hold property separate from their husbands was to break up the harmony of the marriage relation, we know practically that it has not worked that way. We know that as we have made women independent, recognized her legal existence as a wife, secured her rights, and not made her the mere slave of her husband, it has elevated her. We know that instead of disturbing the marriage relation, it has improved it constantly; and I believe that the woman has the same natural right to a voice in this Government that the man has. If we believe, in the theory of our Government that must be so. We say that all men, all human beings, are created equal; that they are endowed by their Creator with certain inalienable rights, and among these are life, liberty, and the pursuit of happiness, and that to attain these rights Governments are instituted, which derive their just powers from the consent of the governed; and yet here are one-half of the people of the United States who have no power to give their consent or their dissent. The theory of our Government is expressly violated in regard to woman. I believe that as you make woman the equal of man in regard to civil rights, rights of property, rights of person, political rights, you elevate her, you make her happier; and as you do that you elevate the male sex, her husband, her son, her brother, and her father.

Mr. BAYARD. Mr. President, it would seem scarcely credible that in the Senate of the United States an abrupt and sudden change in so fundamental a relation as that borne by the two sexes to our system of Government should be proposed as an "experiment," and that it should be gravely recommended that a newly organized Territory under act of Congress should be set aside for this "experiment" which is indirect, grossly irreverent disregard of all that we have known as our rule, our great fundamental rule, in organizing a government of laws, whether colonial, State, or Federal, in this country.

I frankly say, Mr. President, that which strikes me most forcibly is the gross irreverence of this proposition, its utter disregard of that Divine will by which man and woman were created different, physically, intellectually, and morally, and in defiance of which we are now to have this poor, weak, futile attempt of man to set up his schemes of amelioration in defiance of all that we have read, of every tradition, of every revelation, of all human experience, enlightened as it has been by Divine permission. It seems to me that to introduce so grave a subject as this, to spring it here upon the Senate without notice in the shape of an amendment to a pending measure, to propose thus to experiment with the great laws that lie at the very foundation of human society, and to do it for the most part in the trivial tone which we have witnessed during this debate, is not only mortifying, but it renders one almost hopeless of the permanence of our Government if this is to be the example set by one of the Houses of Congress, that which claims to be more sedate and deliberate, if it proposes in this light and perfunctory way to deal with questions of this grave nature and import.

Sir, there is no time at present for that preparation which such a subject demands at the hands of any sensible man, mindful of his responsibilities, who seeks to deal with it.

This is an attempt to disregard laws promulgated by the Almighty Himself. It is irreverent legislation in the simplest and strongest sense of the word. Nay, sir, not only so, but it is a step in defiance of the laws of revealed religion as given to men. If there be one institution which it seems to me has affected the character of this country, which has affected the whole character of modern civilization, the results of which we can but imperfectly trace and but partly recognize, it is the effect of the institution of Christian marriage, the mysterious tie uniting the one man and the one woman until they shall become one and not two persons. It is an institution which is mysterious, which is beyond the reach and the understanding of man, but he certainly can best exhibit his sense of duty and proper obligation when he reverently shall submit to and recognize its wisdom. All such laws as proposed by this amendment are stumbling-blocks and are meant to be stumbling-blocks in the way of that perfect union of the sexes which was intended by the law of Christian marriage.

Under the operation of this amendment what will become of the family, what will become of the family hearthstone around which cluster the very best influences of human education? You will have a family with two heads—a "house divided against itself." You will no longer have that healthful and necessary subordination of wife to husband, and that unity of relationship which is required by a true and a real Christian marriage. You will have substituted a system of contention and difference warring against the laws of nature herself, and attempting by these new-fangled, petty, puny, and most contemptible contrivances, organized in defiance of the best lessons of human experience, to confuse, impede, and disarrange the palpable will of the Creator of the world. I can see in this proposition for female suffrage the end of all that home-life and education which are the best nursery for a nation's virtue. I can see in all these attempts to invade the relations between man and wife, to establish differences, to declare those to be two whom God hath declared to be one, elements of chaotic disorder, elements of destruction to all those things which are, after all, our best reliance for a good and a pure and an honest government.

The best protection for the women of America is in the respect and the love which the men of America bear to them. Every man conversant with the practical affairs of life knows that the fact, that the mere fact that it is a woman who seeks her rights in a court of justice alone gives her an advantage over her contestant which few men are able to resist. I would put it to any man who has practiced law in the courts of this country; let him stand before a jury composed only of men, let the case be tried only by men; let all the witnesses be men; and the plaintiff or the defendant be a woman, and if you choose to add to that, even more unprotected than women generally are, a widow or an orphan, and does not every one recognize the difficulty, not to find protection for her rights, but the difficulty to induce the men who compose the juries of America to hold the balance of justice steadily enough to insure that the rights of others are not invaded by the force of sympathy for her sex? These are common every-day illustrations. They could be multiplied *ad infinitum*.

Mr. President, there never was a greater mistake, there never was a false fact stated than that the women of America need any protection further than the love borne to them by their fellow-countrymen. Every right, every privilege, many that men do not attempt, many that men cannot hope for, are theirs most freely. Do not imperil the advantages which they have; do not attempt in this hasty, ill-considered, shallow way to interfere with the relations which are founded upon the laws of nature herself. Depend upon it, Mr. President, man's wisdom is best shown by humble attention, by humble obedience to the great laws of nature; and those discoveries which have led men to their chiefest enjoyment and greatest advantages have been from the great minds of those who did lay their ears near the heart of nature, listened to its beatings, and did not attempt to correct God's handiwork by their own futile attempts at improvement.

4-C

Are Women Enfranchised by the Fourteenth and Fifteenth Amendments?

On December 19, 1870, Victoria Woodhull, on her own initiative, submitted a memorial to the House and Senate in which she argued that women were citizens, and as such were protected from disfranchisement by the Fourteenth and Fifteenth Amendments. Her memorial was referred to the House Judiciary Committee and three weeks later she offered an address, which may have been written by Congressman Benjamin F. Butler, an able lawyer and a suffragist. The argument contained in these documents had already been suggested by Francis Minor of St. Louis, Missouri. It was welcomed by members of the National Woman Suffrage Association, who continued to use it until 1875 when the Supreme Court in *Minor v. Happerset* declared that it was not valid (See Document 4-d).

Document†

The Memorial of Victoria C. Woodhull.

To the Honorable the Senate and House of Representatives of the United States in Congress assembled, respectfully showeth:

That she was born in the State of Ohio, and is above the age of twenty-one years; that she has resided in the State of New York during the past three years; that she is still a resident thereof, and that she is a citizen of the United States, as declared by the XIV. Article of the Amendments to the Constitution of the United States.

That since the adoption of the XV. Article of the Amendments to the Constitution, neither the State of New York nor any other State, nor any Territory, has passed any law to abridge the right of any citizen of the United

†From: Susan B. Anthony et al., *History of Woman Suffrage* (Rochester: Susan B. Anthony, 1881), vol. II, pp. 443-48.

States to vote, as established by said article, neither on account of sex or otherwise. That, nevertheless, the right to vote is denied to women citizens of the United States by the operation of Election Laws in the several States and Territories, which laws were enacted prior to the adoption of the said XV. Article, and which are inconsistent with the Constitution as amended, and, therefore, are void and of no effect; but which, being still enforced by the said States and Territories, render the Constitution inoperative as regards the right of women citizens to vote:

And whereas, Article VI., Section 2, declares "That this Constitution and the laws of the United States which shall be made in pursuance thereof, and all treaties made, or which shall be made, under the authority of the United States, shall be the supreme law of the land; and all judges in every State shall be bound thereby, anything in the Constitution and laws of any State to the contrary, notwithstanding."

And whereas, no distinction between citizens is made in the Constitution of the United States on account of sex; but the XV. Article of Amendments to it provides that "No State shall make or enforce any law which shall abridge the privileges and immunities of citizens of the United States, nor deny to any person within its jurisdiction the equal protection of the laws."

And whereas, Congress has power to make laws which shall be necessary and proper for carrying into execution all powers vested by the Constitution in the Government of the United States; and to make or alter all regulations in relation to holding elections for senators or representatives, and especially to enforce, by appropriate legislation, the provisions of the said XIV. Article:

And whereas, the continuance of the enforcement of said local election laws, denying and abridging the right of citizens to vote on account of sex, is a grievance to your memorialist and to various other persons, citizens of the United States.

Therefore, your memorialist would most respectfully petition your honorable bodies to make such laws as in the wisdom of Congress shall be necessary and proper for carrying into execution the right vested by the Constitution in the citizens of the United States to vote, without regard to sex.

And your memorialist will ever pray.

New York City, Dec. 19, 1870.   VICTORIA C. WOODHULL.

Address of Victoria C. Woodhull January 11, 1871.

To the Honorable the Judiciary Committee of the House of Representatives of the Congress of the United States:

Having most respectfully memorialized Congress for the passage of such laws as in its wisdom shall seem necessary and proper to carry into effect the rights vested by the Constitution of the United States in the citizens to vote, without regard to sex, I beg leave to submit to your honorable body the following in favor of my prayer in said memorial which has been referred to your Committee.

The public law of the world is founded upon the conceded fact that sovereignty can not be forfeited or renounced. The sovereign power of this country is perpetually in the politically organized people of the United States, and can neither be relinquished nor abandoned by any portion of them. The people in this republic who confer sovereignty are its citizens: in a monarchy the people are the subjects of sovereignty. All citizens of a republic by rightful act or implication confer sovereign power. All people of a monarchy are subjects who exist under its supreme shield and enjoy its immunities. The subject of a monarch takes municipal immunities from the sovereign as a gracious favor; but the woman citizen of this country has the inalienable "sovereign" right of self-government in her own proper person. Those who look upon woman's status by the dim light of the common law, which unfolded itself under the feudal and military institutions that establish right upon physical power, can not find any analogy in the status of the woman citizen of this country, where the broad sunshine of our Constitution has enfranchised all.

As sovereignty can not be forfeited, relinquished, or abandoned, those from whom it flows—the citizens—are equal in conferring the power, and should be equal in the enjoyment of its benefits and in the exercise of its rights and privileges. One portion of citizens have no power to deprive another portion of rights and privileges such as are possessed and exercised by themselves. The male citizen has no more right to deprive the female citizen of the free, public, political, expression of opinion than the female citizen has to deprive the male citizen thereof.

The sovereign will of the people is expressed in our written Constitution, which is the supreme law of the land. The Constitution makes no distinction of sex. The Constitution defines a woman born or naturalized in the United States, and subject to the jurisdiction thereof, to be a citizen. It recognizes the right of citizens to vote. It declares that the right of citizens of the United States to vote shall not be denied or abridged by the United States or by any State on account of "race, color, or previous condition of servitude."

Women, white and black, belong to races, although to different races. A race of people comprises all the people, male and female. The right to vote can not be denied on account of race. All people included in the term race have the right to vote, unless otherwise prohibited. Women of all races are white, black, or some intermediate color. Color comprises all people, of all races and both sexes. The right to vote can not be denied on account of color. All people included in the term color have the right to vote unless otherwise prohibited.

With the right to vote sex has nothing to do. Race and color include all people of both sexes. All people of both sexes have the right to vote, unless prohibited by special limiting terms less comprehensive than race or color. No such limiting terms exist in the Constitution. Women, white and black, have from time immemorial groaned under what is properly termed in the Constitution "previous condition of servitude." Women are the equals of men before the law, and are equal in all their rights as citizens. Women are debarred from voting in some parts of the United States, although they are allowed to exercise that right elsewhere. Women were formerly permitted to vote in places where they are now debarred therefrom. The naturalization laws of the United States expressly provide for the naturalization of women. But the right to vote has only lately been definitely declared by the Constitution to be inalienable, under three distinct conditions—in all of which woman is clearly embraced.

The citizen who is taxed should also have a voice in the subject matter of taxation. "No taxation without representation" is a right which was fundamentally established at the very birth of our country's independence; and by what ethics does any free government impose taxes on women without giving them a voice upon the subject or a participation in the public declaration as to how and by whom these taxes shall be applied for common public use? Women are free to own and to control property, separate and free from males, and they are held responsible in their own proper persons, in every particular, as well as men, in and out of court. Women have the same inalienable right to life, liberty, and the pursuit of happiness that men have. Why have they not this right politically, as well as men?

Women constitute a majority of the people of this country—they hold vast portions of the nation's wealth and pay a proportionate share of the taxes. They are intrusted with the most vital responsibilities of society; they bear, rear, and educate men; they train and mould their characters; they inspire the noblest impulses in men; they often hold the accumulated fortunes of a man's life for the safety of the family and as guardians of the infants, and yet they are debarred from uttering any opinion by public vote, as to the management by public servants of these interests; they are the secret counselors, the best advisers, the most devoted aids in the most trying periods of men's lives, and yet men shrink from trusting them in the common questions of ordinary politics. Men trust women in the market, in the shop, on the highway and railroad, and in all other public places and assemblies, but when they propose to carry a slip of paper with a name upon it to the polls, they fear them. Nevertheless, as citizens, women have the right to vote; they are part and parcel of that great element in which the sovereign power of the land had birth; and it is by usurpation only that men debar them from this right. The American nation, in its march onward and upward, can not publicly choke the intellectual and political activity of half its citizens by narrow statues. The will of the entire people is the true basis of republican government, and a free expression of that will by the public vote of all citizens, without distinctions of race, color, occupation, or sex, is the only means by which that will can be ascertained. As the world has advanced into civilization and culture; as mind has risen in its dominion over matter; as the principle of justice and moral right has gained sway, and merely physical organized power has yielded thereto; as the might of right has supplanted the right of might, so have the rights of women become more fully recognized, and that recognition is the result of the development of the minds of men, which through the ages she has polished, and thereby heightened the lustre of civilization.

It was reserved for our great country to recognize by constitutional enactment that political equality of all citizens which religion, affection, and common sense should have long since accorded; it was reserved for America to sweep away the mist of prejudice and ignorance, and that chivalric condescension of a darker age, for in the language of Holy Writ, "The night is far spent, the day is at hand, let us therefore cast off the work of darkness and let us put on the armor of light. Let us walk honestly as in the day." It may be argued against the proposition that there still remains upon the statute books of some States the word "male" to an exclusion; but as the Constitution, in its paramount character, can only be read by the light of the established principle, *ita lex Scripta est*, and as the subject of sex is not mentioned, and the Constitution is not limited either in terms or by necessary implication in the general rights of citizens to vote, this right can not be limited on account of anything in the spirit of inferior or previous enactments upon a subject which is not mentioned in the supreme law. A different construction would destroy a vested right in a portion of the citizens, and this no legislature has a right to do without compensation, and nothing can compensate a citizen for the loss of his or her suffrage—its value is equal to the value of life. Neither can it be presumed that women are to be kept from the polls as a mere police regulation: it is to be hoped, at least, that police regulations in their case need not be very active. The effect of the amendments to the Constitution must be to annul the power over this subject in the States, whether past, present, or future, which is contrary to the amendments. The amendments would even arrest the action of the Supreme Court in cases pending before it prior to their adoption, and operate as an absolute prohibition to the exercise of any other jurisdiction than merely to dismiss the suit. 3 Dall., 382: 6 Wheaton, 405; 9 ib., 868; 3d Circ. Pa., 1832.

And if the restrictions contained in the Constitution as to color, race or servitude, were designed to limit the State governments in reference to their own citizens, and were intended to operate also as restrictions on the federal power, and to prevent interference with the rights of the State and its citizens, how, then, can the State restrict citizens of the United States in the exercise of rights not mentioned in any restrictive clause in reference to actions on the part of those citizens having reference solely to the necessary functions of the General Government, such as the election of representatives and senators to Congress, whose election the Constitution expressly gives Congress the power to regulate? S.C., 1847: Fox vs. Ohio, 5 Howard, 410.

Your memorialist complains of the existence of State laws, and prays Congress, by appropriate legislation, to declare them, as they are, annulled, and to give vitality to the Constitution under its power to make and alter the regulations of the States contravening the same.

It may be urged in opposition that the courts have power, and should declare upon this subject. The Supreme Court has the power, and it would be its duty so to declare the law: but the court will not do so unless a determination of such point as shall arise make it necessary to the determination of a controversy, and hence a case must be presented in which there can be no rational doubt. All this would subject the aggrieved parties to much dilatory, expensive and needless litigation, which your memorialist prays your honorable body to dispense with by appropriate legislation, as there can be no purpose in special arguments *"ad inconvenienti,"* enlarging or contracting the import of the language of the Constitution.

Therefore, Believing firmly in the right of citizens to freely approach those in whose hands their destiny is placed under the Providence of God, your memorialist has frankly, but humbly, appealed to you, and prays that the wisdom of Congress may be moved to action in this matter for the benefit and the increased happiness of our beloved country.

4-d

The Supreme Court Says Women are Citizens— But Not Voters

Virginia Louisa Minor was the first woman in Missouri to take a public stand in favor of woman suffrage. Her husband, Francis Minor, was a lawyer, and he was the first person to argue that women were enfranchised by the equal protection clause of the Fourteenth Amendment. In 1872 Mrs. Minor and her husband filed suit against a St. Louis registrar who had refused to allow her to register. The lower court held against the Minors, who then appealed to the Supreme Court of the United States. In 1875 the Court handed down a unanimous decision holding that suffrage was not coextensive with citizenship and that the political rights of women were to be decided by the states. The opinion did say, "If the law is wrong, it ought to be changed," but added that "the power for that is not with us."

After this ruling the National Woman Suffrage Association felt it had no alternative but to make a proposed amendment (introduced by Senator Sergeant in 1874 and for years referred to as "the Sixteenth Amendment") the focus of its agitation.

Document†

Minor v. Happerset

The CHIEF JUSTICE delivered the opinion of the court.

The question is presented in this case, whether, since the adoption of the fourteenth amendment, a woman, who is a citizen of the United States and of the State of Missouri, is a voter in that State, notwithstanding the provision of the constitution and laws of the State, which confine the right of suffrage to men alone. We might, perhaps, decide the case upon other grounds, but this question is fairly made. From the opinion we find that it was the only one decided in the court below, and it is the only one which has been argued here. The case was undoubtedly brought to this court for the sole purpose of having that question decided by us, and in view of the evident propriety there

†From: *Minor v. Happerset,* [U.S. Reports], 21 Wallace 162 (1875).

is of having it settled, so far as it can be by such a decision, we have concluded to waive all other considerations and proceed at once to its determination.

It is contended that the provisions of the constitution and laws of the State of Missouri which onfine the right of suffrage and registration therefor to men, are in violation of the Constitution of the United States, and therefore void. The argument is, that as a woman, born or naturalized in the United States and subject to the jurisdiction thereof, is a citizen of the United States and of the State in which she resides, she has the right of suffrage as one of the privileges and immunities of her citizenship, which the State cannot by its laws or constitution abridge.

There is no doubt that women may be citizens. They are persons, and by the fourteenth amendment "all persons born or naturalized in the United States and subject to the jurisdiction thereof" are expressly declared to be "citizens of the United States and of the State wherein they reside." But, in our opinion, it did not need this amendment to give them that position. Before its adoption the Constitution of the United States did not in terms prescribe who should be citizens of the United States or of the several States, yet there were necessarily such citizens without such provision. There cannot be a nation without a people. The very idea of a political community, such as a nation is, implies an association of persons for the promotion of their general welfare. Each one of the persons associated becomes a member of the nation formed by the association. He owes it allegiance and is entitled to its protection. Allegiance and protection are, in this connection, reciprocal obligations. The one is a compensation for the other; allegiance for protection and protection for allegiance.

For convenience it has been found necessary to give a name to this membership. The object is to designate by a title the person and the relation he bears to the nation. For this purpose the words "subject," "inhabitant," and "citizen" have been used, and the choice between them is sometimes made to depend upon the form of the government. Citizen is now more commonly employed, however, and as it has been considered better suited to the description of one living under a republican government, it was adopted by nearly all of the States upon their separation from Great Britain, and was afterwards adopted in the Articles of Confederation and in the Constitution of the United States. When used in this sense it is understood as conveying the idea of membership of a nation, and nothing more.

To determine, then, who were citizens of the United States before the adoption of the amendment it is necessary to ascertain what persons originally associated themselves together to form the nation, and what were afterwards admitted to membership.

Looking at the Constitution itself we find that it was ordained and established by "the people of the United States," and then going further back, we find that these were the people of the several States that had before dissolved the political bands which connected them with Great Britain, and assumed a separate and equal station among the powers of the earth, and that had by Articles of Confederation and Perpetual Union, in which they took the name of "the United States of America," entered into a firm league of friendship with each other for their common defence, the security of their liberties and their mutual and general welfare, binding themselves to assist each other against all force offered to or attack made upon them, or any of them, on account of religion, sovereignty, trade, or any other pretence whatever.

Whoever, then, was one of the people of either of these States when the Constitution of the United States was adopted, became *ipso facto* a citizen—a member of the nation created by its adoption. He was one of the persons associating together to form the nation, and was, consequently, one of its original citizens. As to this there has never been a doubt. Disputes have arisen as to whether or not certain persons or certain classes of persons were part of the people at the time, but never as to their citizenship if they were.

Additions might always be made to the citizenship of the United States in two ways: first, by birth, and second, by naturalization. This is apparent from the Constitution itself, for it provides that "no person except a natural-born citizen, or a citizen of the United States at the time of the adoption of the Constitution, shall be eligible to the office of President," and that Congress shall have power "to establish a uniform rule of naturalization." Thus new citizens may be born or they may be created by naturalization.

The Constitution does not, in words, say who shall be natural-born citizens. Resort must be had elsewhere to ascertain that. At common-law, with the nomenclature of which the framers of the Constitution were familiar, it was never doubted that all children born in a country of parents who were its citizens became themselves, upon their birth, citizens also. These were natives, or natural-born citizens, as distinguished from aliens or foreigners. Some authorities go further and include as citizens children born within the jurisdiction without reference to the citizenship of their parents. As to this class there have been doubts, but never as to the first. For the purposes of this case it is not necessary to solve these doubts. It is sufficient for everything we have now to consider that all children born of citizen parents within the jurisdiction are themselves citizens. The words "all children" are certainly as comprehensive, when used in this connection, as "all persons," and if females are included in the last they must be in the first. That they are included in the last is not denied. In fact the whole argument of the plaintiffs proceeds upon that idea.

Under the power to adopt a uniform system of naturalization Congress, as early as 1790, provided "that any alien, being a free white person," might be admitted as a citizen of the United States, and that the children of such persons so naturalized, dwelling within the United States, being under twenty-one years of age at the time of such naturalization, should also be considered citizens of the United States, and that the children of citizens of the United States that might be born beyond the sea, or out of the limits of the United States, should be considered as natural-born citizens. These provisions thus enacted have, in substance, been retained in all the naturalization laws adopted since. In 1855, however, the last provision was somewhat extended, and all persons theretofore born or thereafter to be born out of the limits of the jurisdiction of the United States, whose fathers were, or should be at the time of their birth, citizens of the United States, were declared to be citizens also.

As early as 1804 it was enacted by Congress that when any alien who had declared his intention to become a citizen in the manner provided by law died before he was actually naturalized, his widow and children should be considered as citizens of the United States, and entitled to all rights and privileges as such upon taking the necessary oath and in 1855 it was further provided that any woman who might lawfully be naturalized under the existing laws, married, or who should be married to a citizen of the United States, should be deemed and taken to be a citizen.

From this it is apparent that from the commencement of the legislation upon this subject alien women and alien minors could be made citizens by naturalization, and we think it will not be contended that this would have been done if it had not been supposed that native women and native minors were already citizens by birth.

But if more is necessary to show that women have always been considered as citizens the same as men, abundant proof is to be found in the legislative and judicial history of the country. Thus, by the Constitution, the judicial power of the United States is made to extend to controversies between citizens of different States. Under this it has been uniformly held that the citizenship necessary to give the courts of the United States jurisdiction of a cause must be affirmatively shown on the record. Its existence as a fact may be put in issue and tried. If found not to exist the case must be dismissed. Notwithstanding this the records of the courts are full of cases in which the jurisdiction depends upon the citizenship of women, and not one can be found, we think, in which objection was made on that account. Certainly none can be found in which it has been held that women could not sue or be sued in the courts of the United States. Again, at the time of the adoption of the Constitution, in many of the States (and in some probably now) aliens could not inherit or transmit inheritance. There are a multitude of cases to be found in which the question has been presented whether a woman was or was not an alien, and as such capable or incapable of inheritance, but in no one has it been insisted that she was not a citizen because she was a woman. On the contrary, her right to citizenship has been in all cases assumed. The only question has been whether, in the particular case under consideration, she had availed herself of the right.

In the legislative department of the government similar proof will be found. Thus, in the pre-emption laws, a widow, "being a citizen of the United States," is allowed to make settlement on the public lands and purchase upon the terms specified, and women, "being citizens of the United States," are permitted to avail themselves of the benefit of the homestead law.

Other proof of like character might be found, but certainly more cannot be necessary to establish the fact that sex has never been made one of the elements of citizenship in the United States. In this respect men have never had an advantage over women. The same laws precisely apply to both. The fourteenth amendment did not affect the citizenship of women any more than it did of men. In this particular, therefore, the rights of Mrs. Minor do not depend upon the amendment. She has always been a citizen from her birth, and entitled to all the privileges and immunities of citizenship. The amendment prohibited the State, of which she is a citizen, from abridging any of her privileges and immunities as a citizen of the United States; but it did not confer citizenship on her. That she had before its adoption.

If the right of suffrage is one of the necessary privileges of a citizen of the United States, then the constitution and laws of Missouri confining it to men are in violation of the Constitution of the United States, as amended, and consequently void. The direct question is, therefore, presented whether all citizens are necessarily voters.

The Constitution does not define the privileges and immunities of citizens. For that definition we must look elsewhere. In this case we need not determine what they are, but only whether suffrage is necessarily one of them.

It certainly is nowhere made so in express terms. The United States has no voters in the States of its own creation. The elective officers of the United States are all elected directly or indirectly by State voters. The members of the House of Representatives are to be chosen by the people of the States, and the electors in each State must have the qualifications requisite for electors of the most numerous branch of the State legislature. Senators are to be chosen by the legislatures of the States, and necessarily the members of the legislature required to make the choice are elected by the voters of the State. Each State must appoint in such manner, as the legislature thereof may direct, the electors to elect the President and Vice-President. The times, places, and manner of holding elections for Senators and Representatives are to be prescribed in each State by the legislature thereof; but Congress may at any time, by law, make or alter such regulations, except as to the place of choosing Senators. It is not necessary to inquire whether this power of supervision thus given to Congress is sufficient to authorize any interference with the State laws prescribing the qualifications of voters, for no such interference has ever been attempted. The power of the State in this particular is certainly supreme until Congress acts.

The amendment did not add to the privileges and immunities of a citizen. It simply furnished an additional guaranty for the protection of such as he already had. No new voters were necessarily made by it. Indirectly it may have had that effect, because it may have increased the number of citizens entitled to suffrage under the constitution and laws of the States, but it operates for this purpose, if at all, through the States and the State laws, and not directly upon the citizen.

It is clear, therefore, we think, that the Constitution has not added the right of suffrage to the privileges and immunities of citizenship as they existed at the time it was adopted. This makes it proper to inquire whether suffrage was coextensive with the citizenship of the States at the time of its adoption. If it was, then it may with force be argued that suffrage was one of the rights which belonged to citizenship, and in the enjoyment of which every citizen must be protected. But if it was not, the contrary may with propriety be assumed.

When the Federal Constitution was adopted, all the States, with the exception of Rhode Island and Connecticut, had constitutions of their own. These two continued to act under their charters from the Crown. Upon an examination of those constitutions we find that in no State were all citizens permitted to vote. Each State determined for itself who should have that power.

. . . .

In this condition of the law in respect to suffrage in the several States it cannot for a moment be doubted that if it had been intended to make all citizens of the United States voters, the framers of the Constitution would not have left it to implication. So important a change in the condition of citizenship as it actually existed, if intended, would have been expressly declared.

But if further proof is necessary to show that no such change was intended, it can easily be found both in and out of the Constitution. By Article 4, section 2, it is provided that "the citizens of each State shall be entitled to all the privileges and immunities of citizens in the several States." If suffrage is necessarily a part of citizenship, then the citizens of each State must be entitled to vote in the several States precisely as their citizens are. This is more than asserting that they may change their residence and become citizens of the State and thus be voters. It goes to the extent of insisting that while retaining their original citizenship they may vote in any State. This, we think, has never been claimed. And again, by the very terms of the amendment we have been considering (the fourteenth), "Representatives shall be apportioned among the several States according to their respective numbers, counting the whole number of persons in each State, excluding Indians not taxed. But when the right to vote at any election for the choice of electors for President and Vice-President of the United States, representatives in Congress, the executive and judicial officers of a State, or the members of the legislature thereof, is denied to any of the male inhabitants of such State, being twenty-one years of age and citizens of the United States, or in any way abridged, except for participation in the rebellion, or other crimes, the basis of representation therein shall be reduced in the proportion which the number of such male citizens shall bear to the whole number of male citizens twenty-one years of age in such State." Why this, if it was not in the power of the legislature to deny the right of suffrage to some male inhabitants? And if suffrage was necessarily one of the absolute rights of citizenship, why confine the operation of the limitation to male inhabitants? Women and children are, as we have seen, "persons." They are counted in the enumeration upon which the apportionment is to be made, but if they were necessarily voters because of their citizenship unless clearly excluded, why inflict the penalty for the exclusion of males alone? Clearly, no such form of words would have been selected to express the idea here indicated if suffrage was the absolute right of all citizens.

And still again, after the adoption of the fourteenth amendment, it was deemed necessary to adopt a fifteenth, as follows: "The right of citizens of the United States to vote shall not be denied or abridged by the United States, or by any State, on account of race, color, or previous condition of servitude." The fourteenth amendment had already provided that no State should make or enforce any law which should abridge the privileges or immunities of citizens of the United States. If suffrage was one of these privileges or immunities, why amend the Constitution to prevent its being denied on account of race, &c.? Nothing is more evident than that the greater must include the less, and if all were already protected why go through with the form of amending the Constitution to protect a part?

It is true that the United States guarantees to every State a republican form of government. It is also true that no State can pass a bill of attainder, and that no person can be deprived of life, liberty, or property without due process of law. All these several provisions of the Constitution must be construed in connection with the other parts of the instrument, and in the light of the surrounding circumstances.

The guaranty is of a republican form of government. No particular government is designated as republican, neither is the exact form to be guaranteed, in any manner especially designated. Here, as in other parts of the instrument, we are compelled to resort elsewhere to ascertain what was intended.

The guaranty necessarily implies a duty on the part of the States themselves to provide such a government. All the States had governments when the Constitution was adopted. In all the people participated to some extent, through their representatives elected in the manner specially provided. These governments the Constitution did not change. They were accepted precisely as they were, and it is, therefore, to be presumed that they were such as it was the duty of the States to provide. Thus we have unmistakable evidence of what was republican in form, within the meaning of that term as employed in the Constitution.

As has been seen, all the citizens of the States were not invested with the right of suffrage. In all, save perhaps New Jersey, this right was only bestowed upon men and not upon all of them. Under these circumstances it is certainly now too late to contend that a government is not republican, within the meaning of this guaranty in the Constitution, because women are not made voters.

The same may be said of the other provisions just quoted. Women were excluded from suffrage in nearly all the States by the express provision of their constitutions and laws. If that had been equivalent to a bill of attainder, certainly its abrogation would not have been left to implication. Nothing less than express language would have been employed to effect so radical a change. So also of the amendment which declares that no person shall be deprived of life, liberty, or property without due process of law, adopted as it was as early as 1791. If suffrage was intended to be included within its obligations, language better adapted to express that intent would most certainly have been employed. The right of suffrage, when granted, will be protected. He who has it can only be deprived of it by due process of law, but in order to claim protection he must first show that he has the right.

But we have already sufficiently considered the proof found upon the inside of the Constitution. That upon the outside is equally effective.

The Constitution was submitted to the States for adoption in 1787, and was ratified by nine States in 1788, and finally by the thirteen original States in 1790. Vermont was the first new States admitted to the Union, and it came in under a constitution which conferred the right of suffrage only upon men of the full age of twenty-one years, having resided in the State for the space of one whole year next before the election, and who were of quiet and peaceable behavior. This was in 1791. The next year, 1792, Kentucky followed with a constitution confining the right of suffrage to free male citizens of the age of twenty-one years who had resided in the State two years or in the county in which they offered to vote one year next before the election. Then followed Tennessee, in 1796, with voters of freemen of the age of twenty-one years and upwards, possessing a freehold in the county wherein they may vote, and being inhabitants of the State or freemen being inhabitants of any one county in the State six months immediately preceding the day of election. But we need not particularize further. No new State has ever been admitted to the Union which has conferred the right of suffrage upon women, and this has never been considered a valid objection to her admission. On the contrary, as is claimed in the argument, the right of suffrage was withdrawn from women as early as 1807 in the State of New Jersey, without any attempt to obtain the interference of the United States to prevent it. Since then the governments of the insurgent States have been reorganized under a requirement that before their representatives could be admitted to seats in Congress they must have adopted new constitutions, republican in form. In no one of these constitutions was suffrage conferred upon women, and yet the States have all been restored to their original position as States in the Union.

Besides this, citizenship has not in all cases been made a condition precedent to the enjoyment of the right of suffrage. Thus, in Missouri, persons of foreign birth, who have declared their intention to become citizens of the United States, may under certain circumstances vote. The same provision is to be found in the constitutions of Alabama, Arkansas, Florida, Georgia, Indiana, Kansas, Minnesota, and Texas.

Certainly, if the courts can consider any question settled, this is one. For nearly ninety years the people have acted upon the idea that the Constitution, when it conferred citizenship, did not necessarily confer the right of suffrage. If uniform practice long continued can settle the construction of so important an instrument as the Constitution of the United

States confessedly is, most certainly it has been done here. Our province is to decide what the law is, not to declare what it should be.

We have given this case the careful consideration its importance demands. If the law is wrong, it ought to be changed; but the power for that is not with us. The arguments addressed to us bearing upon such a view of the subject may perhaps be sufficient to induce those having the power, to make the alteration, but they ought not to be permitted to influence our judgment in determining the present rights of the parties now litigating before us. No argument as to woman's need of suffrage can be considered. We can only act upon her rights as they exist. It is not for us to look at the hardship of withholding. Our duty is at an end if we find it is within the power of a State to withhold.

Being unanimously of the opinion that the Constitution of the United States does not confer the right of suffrage upon any one, and that the constitutions and laws of the several States which commit that important trust to men alone are not necessarily void, we

AFFIRM THE JUDGMENT.

4-e

Women's Declaration of Rights

The centennial celebration of 1876 was planned without reference to women, and no place had been provided for them on the program. Susan Anthony and Elizabeth Stanton decided that a protest was in order. They devised a Women's Declaration of Rights, which they planned to present, invited or not. In the *History of Woman Suffrage* they recorded how they went about it.

Document†

That historic Fourth of July dawned at last, one of the most oppressive days of that terribly heated season. Susan B. Anthony, Matilda Joslyn Gage, Sara Andrews Spencer, Lillie Devereux Blake and Phoebe W. Couzins made their way through the crowds under the broiling sun to Independence Square, carrying the Woman's Declaration of Rights. This declaration had been handsomely engrossed by one of their number, and signed by the oldest and most prominent advocates of woman's enfranchisement. Their tickets of admission proved open sesame through the military and all other barriers, and a few moments before the opening of the ceremonies, these women found themselves within the precincts from which most of their sex were excluded.

The declaration of 1776 was read by Richard Henry Lee, of Virginia, about whose family clusters so much of historic fame. The close of his reading was deemed the appropriate moment for the presentation of the woman's declaration. Not quite sure how their approach might be met—not quite certain if at this final moment they would be permitted to reach the presiding officer—those ladies arose and made their way down the aisle. The bustle of preparation for the Brazilian hymn covered their advance. The foreign guests, the military and civil officers who filled the space directly in front of the speaker's stand, courteously made way, while Miss Anthony in fitting words presented the declaration. Mr. Ferry's face paled, as bowing low, with no word, he received the declaration, which thus became part of the day's proceedings; the ladies turned, scattering printed copies, as they deliberately walked down the platform. On every side eager hands were stretched; men stood on seats and asked for them, while General Hawley, thus defied and beaten in his audacious denial to women the right to present their declaration, shouted, "Order, order!"

†From: Susan B. Anthony et al., *History of Woman Suffrage* (Rochester: Susan B. Anthony, 1881), vol. III, pp. 31-35.

Passing out, these ladies made their way to a platform erected for the musicians in front of Independence Hall. Here on this old historic ground, under the shadow of Washington's statue, back of them the old bell that proclaimed "liberty to all the land, and all the inhabitants thereof," they took their places, and to a listening, applauding crowd, Miss Anthony read* the Declaration of Rights for Women by the National Woman Suffrage Association, July 4, 1876:

While the nation is buoyant with patriotism, and all hearts are attuned to praise, it is with sorrow we come to strike the one discordant note, on this one-hundredth anniversary of our country's birth. When subjects of kings, emperors, and czars, from the old world join in our national jubilee, shall the women of the republic refuse to lay their hands with benedictions on the nation's head? Surveying America's exposition, surpassing in magnificence those of London, Paris, and Vienna, shall we not rejoice at the success of the youngest rival among the nations of the earth? May not our hearts, in unison with all, swell with pride at our great achievements as a people; our free speech, free press, free schools, free church, and the rapid progress we have made in material wealth, trade, commerce and the inventive arts? And we do rejoice in the success, thus far, of our experiment of self-government. Our faith is firm and unwavering in the broad principles of human rights proclaimed in 1776, not only as abstract truths, but as the corner stones of a republic. Yet we cannot forget, even in this glad hour, that while all men of every race, and clime, and condition, have been invested with the full rights of citizenship under our hospitable flag, all women still suffer the degradation of disfranchisement.

The history of our country the past hundred years has been a series of assumptions and usurpations of power over woman, in direct opposition to the principles of just government, acknowledged by the United States as its foundation, which are:

First—The natural rights of each individual.

Second—The equality of these rights.

Third—That rights not delegated are retained by the individual.

Fourth—That no person can exercise the rights of others without delegated authority.

Fifth—That the non-use of rights does not destroy them.

And for the violation of these fundamental principles of our government, we arraign our rulers on this Fourth day of July, 1876,—and these are our articles of impeachment:

Bills of attainder have been passed by the introduction of the word "male" into all the State constitutions, denying to women the right of suffrage, and

*During the reading of the declaration to an immense concourse of people, Mrs. Gage stood beside Miss Anthony, and held an umbrella over her head, to shelter her friend from the intense heat of the noonday sun; and thus in the same hour, on opposite sides of old Independence Hall, did the men and women express their opinions on the great principles proclaimed on the natal day of the republic. The declaration was handsomely framed and now hangs in the vice-president's room in the capitol at Washington.

thereby making sex a crime—an exercise of power clearly forbidden in article I, sections 9, 10, of the United States constitution.

The writ of habeas corpus, the only protection against *lettres de cachet* and all forms of unjust imprisonment, which the constitution declares "shall not be suspended, except when in cases of rebellion or invasion the public safety demands it," is held inoperative in every State of the Union, in case of a married woman against her husband—the marital rights of the husband being in all cases primary, and the rights of the wife secondary.

The right of trial by a jury of one's peers was so jealously guarded that States refused to ratify the original constitution until it was guaranteed by the sixth amendment. And yet the women of this nation have never been allowed a jury of their peers—being tried in all cases by men, native and foreign, educated and ignorant, virtuous and vicious. Young girls have been arraigned in our courts for the crime of infanticide; tried, convicted, hanged—victims, perchance, of judge, jurors, advocates—while no woman's voice could be heard in their defense. And not only are women denied a jury of their peers, but in some cases, jury trial altogether. During the war, a woman was tried and hanged by military law, in defiance of the fifth amendment, which specifically declares: "No person shall be held to answer for a capital or otherwise infamous crime, unless on a presentment or indictment of a grand jury, except in cases . . . . of persons in actual service in time of war." During the last presidential campaign, a woman, arrested for voting, was denied the protection of a jury, tried, convicted, and sentenced to a fine and costs of prosecution, by the absolute power of a judge of the Supreme Court of the United States.

Taxation without representation, the immediate cause of the rebellion of the colonies against Great Britain, is one of the grievous wrongs the women of this country have suffered during the century. Deploring war, with all the demoralization that follows in its train, we have been taxed to support standing armies, with their waste of life and wealth. Believing in temperance, we have been taxed to support the vice, crime and pauperism of the liquor traffic. While we suffer its wrongs and abuses infinitely more than man, we have no power to protect our sons against this giant evil. During the temperance crusade, mothers were arrested, fined, imprisoned, for even praying and singing in the streets, while men blockade the sidewalks with impunity, even on Sunday, with their military parades and political processions. Believing in honesty, we are taxed to support a dangerous army of civilians, buying and selling the offices of government and sacrificing the best interests of the people. And, moreover, we are taxed to support the very legislators and judges who make laws, and render decisions adverse to woman. And for refusing to pay such unjust taxation, the houses, lands, bonds, and stock of women have been seized and sold within the present year, thus proving Lord Coke's assertion, that "The very act of taxing a man's property without his consent is, in effect, disfranchising him of every civil right."

Unequal codes for men and women. Held by law a perpetual minor, deemed incapable of self-protection, even in the industries of the world, woman is denied equality of rights. The fact of sex, not the quantity or quality of work, in most cases, decides the pay and position; and because of this injustice thousands of fatherless girls are compelled to choose between a life of shame and starvation. Laws catering to man's vices have created two codes of morals in which penalties are graded according to the political status of the offender. Under such laws, women are fined and imprisoned if found alone in the streets, or in public places of resort, at certain hours. Under the pretense of regulating public morals, police officers seizing the occupants of disreputable houses, march the women in platoons to prison, while the men, partners in their guilt, go free. While making a show of virtue in forbidding the importation of Chinese women on the Pacific coast for immoral purposes, our rulers, in many States, and even under the shadow of the national capitol, are now proposing to legalize the sale of American womanhood for the same vile purposes.

Special legislation for woman has placed us in a most anomalous position. Women invested with the rights of citizens in one section—voters, jurors, office-holders—crossing an imaginary line, are subjects in the next. In some States, a married woman may hold property and transact business in her own name; in others, her earnings belong to her husband. In some States, a woman may testify against her husband, sue and be sued in the courts; in others, she has no redress in case of damage to person, property, or character. In case of divorce on account of adultery in the husband, the innocent wife is held to possess no right to children or property, unless by special decree of the court. But in no State of the Union has the wife the right to her own person, or to any part of the joint earnings of the co-partnership during the life of her husband. In some States women may enter the law schools and practice in the courts; in others they are forbidden. In some universities girls enjoy equal educational advantages with boys, while many of the proudest institutions in the land deny them admittance, though the sons of China, Japan and Africa are welcomed there. But the privileges already granted in the several States are by no means secure. The right of suffrage once exercised by women in certain States and territories has been denied by subsequent legislation. A bill is now pending in congress to disfranchise the women of Utah, thus interfering to deprive United States citizens of the same rights which the Supreme Court has declared the national government powerless to protect anywhere. Laws passed after years of untiring effort, guaranteeing married women certain rights of property, and mothers the custody of their children, have been repealed in States where we supposed all was safe. Thus have our most sacred rights been made the football of legislative caprice, proving that a power which grants as a privilege what by nature is a right, may withhold the same as a penalty when deeming it necessary for its own perpetuation.

Representation of woman has had no place in the nation's thought. Since the incorporation of the thirteen original States, twenty-four have been admitted to the Union, not one of which has recognized woman's right of self-government. On this birthday of our national liberties, July Fourth,

1876, Colorado, like all her elder sisters, comes into the Union with the invidious word "male" in her constitution.

Universal manhood suffrage, by establishing an aristocracy of sex, imposes upon the women of this nation a more absolute and cruel depotism than monarchy; in that, woman finds a political master in her father, husband, brother, son. The aristocracies of the old world are based upon birth, wealth, refinement, education, nobility, brave deeds of chivalry; in this nation, on sex alone; exalting brute force above moral power, vice above virtue, ignorance above education, and the son above the mother who bore him.

The judiciary above the nation has proved itself but the echo of the party in power, by upholding and enforcing laws that are opposed to the spirit and letter of the constitution. When the slave power was dominant, the Supreme Court decided that a black man was not a citizen, because he had not the right to vote; and when the constitution was so amended as to make all persons citizens, the same high tribunal decided that a woman, though a citizen, had not the right to vote. Such vacillating interpretations of constitutional law unsettle our faith in judicial authority, and undermine the liberties of the whole people.

These articles of impeachment against our rulers we now submit to the impartial judgment of the people. To all these wrongs and oppressions woman has not submitted in silence and resignation. From the beginning of the century, when Abigail Adams, the wife of one president and mother of another, said: "We will not hold ourselves bound to obey laws in which we have no voice or representation," until now, woman's discontent has been steadily increasing, culminating nearly thirty years ago in a simultaneous movement among the women of the nation, demanding the right of suffrage. In making our just demands, a higher motive than the pride of sex inspires us; we feel that national safety and stability depend on the complete recognition of the broad principles of our government. Woman's degraded, helpless position is the weak point in our institutions to-day; a disturbing force everywhere, severing family ties, filling our asylums with the deaf, the dumb, the blind; our prisons with criminals, our cities with drunkenness and prostitution; our homes with disease and death. It was the boast of the founders of the republic, that the rights for which they contended were the rights of human nature. If these rights are ignored in the case of one-half the people, the nation is surely preparing for its downfall. Governments try themselves. The recognition of a governing and a governed class is incompatible with the first principles of freedom. Woman has not been a heedless spectator of the events of this century, nor a dull listener to the grand arguments for the equal rights of humanity. From the earliest history of our country woman has shown equal devotion with man to the cause of freedom, and has stood firmly by his side in its defense. Together, they have made this country what it is. Woman's wealth, thought and labor have cemented the stones of every monument man has reared to liberty.

And now, at the close of a hundred years, as the hour-hand of the great clock that marks the centuries points to 1876, we declare our faith in the principles of self-government; our full equality with man in natural rights; that woman was made first for her own happiness, with the absolute right to herself—to all the opportunities and advantages life affords for her complete development; and we deny that dogma of the centuries, incorporated in the codes of all nations—that woman was made for man—her best interests, in all cases, to be sacrificed to his will. We ask of our rulers, at this hour, no special favors, no special privileges, no special legislation. We ask justice, we ask equality, we ask that all the civil and political rights that belong to citizens of the United States, be guaranteed to us and our daughters forever.

The declaration was warmly applauded at many points, and after scattering another large number of printed copies, the delegation hastened to the convention of the National Association.

5-a

"I am a Home-Loving, Law-Abiding, Tax-Paying Woman...."

It was the custom of the National Woman Suffrage Association to hold its annual convention in Washington, and to use the occasion to present suffrage arguments to congressional committees. In January 1880 at a hearing of the Senate Judiciary Committee Mrs. Zerelda G. Wallace, widow of a governor and a congressman, and stepmother of General Lew Wallace, who had identified her as the original of the mother in his best selling novel, *Ben-Hur*, was among those testifying. Long active in the Women's Christian Temperence Union, Mrs. Wallace offered the argument, which would be used increasingly in subsequent years, that the quality of government would be improved if women were admitted to the electorate.

Document†

Remarks by Mrs. Zerelda G. Wallace, of Indiana.

Mrs. WALLACE. Mr. Chairman and gentlemen of the committee: It is scarcely necessary to recite that there is not an effect without a cause. Therefore it would be well for the statesmen of this nation to ask themselves the question, What has brought the women from all parts of this nation to the capital at this time; the wives and mothers, and sisters; the home-loving, law-abiding women? What has been the strong motive that has taken us away from the quiet and comfort of our own homes and brought us before you to-day? As an answer partly to that question, I will read an extract from a speech made by one of Indiana's statesmen, and probably if I tell you his name his sentiments, may have some weight with you. He found out by experience and gave us the benefit of his experience, and it is what we are rapidly learning:

"You can go to meetings; you can vote resolutions; you can attend great demonstrations on the street; but, after all, the only occasion where the American citizen expresses his acts, his opinion, and his power is at the

†From: U.S., Congress, Senate, Judiciary Committee, *Appendix to the Report on Suffrage*, 49th Cong., 1st Sess., S. Rept. 70, pp. 21-22.

ballot-box; and that little ballot that he drops in there is the written sentiment of the times, and it is the power that he has as a citizen of this great Republic."

That is the reason why we are here; that is the reason why we want to vote. We are no seditious women, clamoring for any peculiar rights, but we are patient women. It is not the woman question that brings us before you to-day; it is the human question that underlies this movement among the women of this nation; it is for God, and home, and native land. We love and appreciate our country; we value the institutions of our country. We realize that we owe great obligations to the men of this nation for what they have done. We realize that to their strength we owe the subjugation of all the material forces of the universe which gives us comfort and luxury in our homes. We realize that to their brains we owe the machinery that gives us leisure for intellectual culture and achievement. We realize that it is to their education we owe the opening of our colleges and the establishment of our public schools, which give us these great and glorious privileges.

This movement is the legitimate result of this development, of this enlightenment, and of the suffering that woman has undergone in the ages past. We find ourselves hedged in at every effort we make as mothers for the amelioration of society, as philanthropists, as Christians.

A short time ago I went before the legislature of Indiana with a petition signed by 25,000 women, the best women in the State. I appeal to the memory of Judge McDonald to substantiate the truth of what I say. Judge McDonald knows that I am a home-loving, law-abiding, tax-paying woman of Indiana, and have been for fifty years. When I went before our legislature and found that one hundred of the vilest men in our State, merely by the possession of the ballot, had more influence with the law-makers of our land than the wives and mothers of the nation, it was a revelation that was perfectly startling.

You must admit that in popular government the ballot is the most potent means of all moral and social reforms. As members of society, as those who are deeply interested in the promotion of good morals, of virtue, and of the proper protection of men from the consequences of their own vices, and of the protection of women, too, we are deeply interested in all the social problems with which you have grappled so long unsuccessfully. We do not intend to depreciate your efforts, but you have attempted to do an impossible thing. You have attempted to represent the whole by one-half; and we come to you to-day for a recognition of the fact that humanity is not a unit; that it is a unity; and because we are one-half that go to make up that grand unity we come before you to-day and ask you to recognize our rights as citizens of this Republic.

We know that many of us lay ourselves liable to contumely and ridicule. We have to meet sneers; but we are determined that in the defense of right we will ignore everything but what we feel to be our duty.

We do not come here as agitators, or aimless, dissatisfied, unhappy women by any means; but we come as human beings, recognizing our responsibility to

God for the advantages that have come to us in the development of the ages. We wish to discharge that responsibility faithfully, effectually, and conscientiously, and we cannot do it under our form of government, hedged in as we are by the lack of a power which is such a mighty engine in our form of government for every means of work.

I say to you, then, we come as one-half of the great whole. There is an essential difference in the sexes. Mr. Parkman labored very hard to prove what no one would deny, that there is an essential difference in the sexes, and it is because of that very differentiation, the union of which in home, the recognition of which in society, brings the greatest happiness, the recognition of which in the church brings the greatest power and influence for good, and the recognition of which in the Government would enable us finally, as near as it is possible for humanity, to perfect our form of government. Probably we can never have a perfect form of government, but the nearer we approximate to the divine the nearer will we attain to perfection; and the divine government recognizes neither caste, class, sex, nor nationality. The nearer we approach to that divine ideal the nearer we will come to realizing our hopes of finally securing at least the most perfect form of human government that it is possible for us to secure.

I do not wish to trespass upon your time, but I have felt that this movement is not understood by a great majority of people. They think that we are unhappy, that we are dissatisfied, that we are restive. That is not the case. When we look over the statistics of our State and find that 60 per cent of all the crime is the result of drunkenness; when we find that 60 per cent of the orphan children that fill our pauper homes are the children of drunken parents; when we find that after a certain age the daughters of those fathers who were made paupers and drunkards by the approbation and sanction and under the seal of the Government, go to supply our houses of prostitution, and when we find that the sons of these fathers go to fill up our jails and our penitentiaries, and that the sober, law-abiding men, the pains-taking, economical, and many of them widowed wives of this nation have to pay taxes and bear the expenses incurred by such legislation, do you wonder, gentlemen, that we at least want to try our hand and see what we can do? We may not be able to bring about that Utopian form of government which we all desire, but we can at least make an effort. Under our form of government the ballot is our right; it is just and proper. When you debate about the expediency of any matter you have no right to say that it is inexpedient to do right. Do right and leave the result to God. You will have to decide between one of two things: either you have no claim under our form of Constitution for the privileges which you enjoy, or you will have to say that we are neither citizens nor persons.

Realizing this fact, and the deep interest that we take in the successful issue of this experiment that humanity is making for self-government, and realizing the fact that the ballot never can be given to us under more favorable circumstances, and believing that here on this continent is to be wrought out the great problem of man's ability to govern himself—and when I say man I use the word in the generic sense—that humanity here is to work out the great problems of self-government and development, and recognizing, as I said a few minutes ago, that we are one-half of the great whole, we feel that we ought to be heard when we come before you and make the plea that we make to-day.

5-b

The Making of a Suffragist

Belle Kearney was a Mississippi woman whom Frances Willard drew into active work for the Woman's Christian Temperance Union. In 1900 she published her autobiography, and explained how she came to be a strong suffragist.

Document†

The freedom of my home environment was perfect, but I recognized the fact that there were tremendous limitations of my "personal liberty" outside the family circle. An instance of it soon painfully impressed my consciousness. Three of my brothers, the comrades of my childhood, had become voting citizens. They were manly and generous enough to sympathize with my ballotless condition, but it was the source of many jokes at my expense among them. On a certain election day in November, they mounted their horses and started for the polls. I stood watching them as they rode off in the splendor of their youth and strength. I was full of love and pride for them, but was feeling keenly the disgrace of being a disfranchised mortal, simply on account of having been born a woman,—and that by no volition of my own. Surmising the storm that was raging in my heart, my second brother—who was at home from the West on a visit of over a year's duration—looking at me, smiling and lifting his hat in mock courtesy said: "Good morning, sister. You taught us and trained us in the way we should go. You gave us money from your hard earnings, and helped us to get a start in the world. You are interested infinitely more in good government and understand politics a thousand times better than we, but it is election day and we leave you at home with the idiots and Indians, incapables, paupers, lunatics, criminals and the other women that the authorities in this nation do not deem it proper to trust with the ballot; while we, lordly men, march to the polls and express our opinions in a way that counts."

There was the echo of a general laugh as they rode away. A salute was waved to them and a good-by smiled in return; but my lips were trembling and my eyes were dim with tears. For the first time the fact was apparent that a wide gulf stretched between my brothers and me; that there was a plane, called political equality, upon which we could not stand together. We had the same home, the same parents, the same faculties, the same general

†From: Belle Kearney, *A Slaveholder's Daughter* (St. Louis: The St. Louis Christian Advocate Press, 1900), pp. 111-112.

outlook. We had loved the same things and striven for the same ends and had been equals in all respects. *Now* I was set aside as inferior, inadequate for citizenship, not because of inferior quality or achievement but by an arbitrary discrimination that seemed as unjust as it was unwise. I too had to live under the laws; then why was it not equally my interest and privilege, to elect the officers who were to make and execute them? I was a human being and a citizen, and a self-supporting, producing citizen, yet my government took no cognizance of me except to set me aside with the unworthy and the incapable for whom the state was forced to provide.

That experience made me a woman suffragist, avowed and uncompromising. Deep down in my heart a vow was made that day that never should satisfaction come to me until by personal effort I had helped to put the ballot into the hands of woman. It became a mastering purpose of my life.

6-a

Testimony to the Senate

In January 1896 the Senate Committee on Women Suffrage heard testimony from a number of women. In light of the particularly adamant antisuffragism of most southern members of Congress, the testimony given by a number of southern women on that occasion is interesting. The statements reprinted here are chosen from a number offered by southern and border state women.

Document†

Remarks of Miss Helen Morris Lewis, of North Carolina

The next lady introduced to the committee was Miss Helen Morris Lewis, of North Carolina. She said:

GENTLEMEN OF THE COMMITTEE: I am here in the interests of the women of North Carolina to petition that we be granted equal rights with men. In our State women are accorded no suffrage whatever; they are permitted to hold no political offices, and many of the laws are detrimental to our welfare.

Woman Suffrage It should be the duty of every civilized government to place a safe-guard around individual liberty, by allowing its people to have a voice to protect their interests.

Ambassador Bayard says: "The result of the destruction of personal freedom is the enfeeblement of the moral fiber and the paralysis of individual, intellectual, and moral growth." These remarks were forcibly illustrated to me a short time since. I lost railroad connection and found myself stranded at one of our remote towns. I resolved to make the most of my time by delivering an address on woman suffrage.

To accomplish this purpose it was necessary for me to visit every house in person and acquaint the inmates with my intention.

I found the men on the village square quite intelligent. The idea of giving the ballot to women was a novelty to them, but they soon hobnobbed together in front of the post-office and harangued every phase of the question with much spirit and hilarity. I felt quite encouraged at this wide awake community, and with renewed energy started forth on my tour amid domestic life.

†From: U.S., Congress, Senate, Committee on Woman Suffrage, *Report of the Hearing Before the Committee on Woman Suffrage,* 54th Cong., 1st sess., Document no. 157, pp. 3-23.

Have you ever visited the poorhouses of our great cities and noticed the pallid hopelessness, the sodden indifference depicted on every countenance?

Well, in an intensified degree was that hopelessness and indifference written in every line of the women's faces I met that day. They were all very poor; they had swarms of children; they were yellow and skinny, hollow-eyed and lantern-jawed, and their hair grew like drought-smitten timothy. Into each separate head I hammered woman suffrage for a solid half hour, dwelling upon the advantages it would bring to their condition. But it was pitiful to observe the feeble ray of intelligence that struggled through their torpid brains. Their bovine vacuity of expression betokened lives devoid of all interest, much less enlightenment. Imprisoned within the walls of homes that contained no comforts, much less luxuries, even the joys that should accompany motherhood had been perverted into sorrow and bitterness.

I contrasted the lives of the men on the square with those of the women. The butcher, the blacksmith, the shoemaker, amid all their grime and drudgery, had an air of self-respect; they felt that they were of importance in the world; they met together, talked on the vital questions of the nation, had ambitions as great as those of Cardinal Wolsey. The men never talked to the women, but went home only to gobble and sleep. Their wives' opinions were perfectly worthless, so they were left to a withering decay of their mental faculties.

When I ponder on the cheerful insensibility of men to the shadowed existence of women, it reminds me of an incident connected with a friend who was ill. Her little boy was rubbing her arm, when she moaned, "Oh, Tommy, mamma's so sorry she's such a trouble to you!" Tommy cheerfully replied, "Never mind, mamma; we doesn't care how much you suffer so long as you is just alive." [Laughter.] Such men as these are but Tommys of a larger growth; they don't care how much we suffer; they think women have sufficient privileges given them in being allowed to be just alive. Now, gentlemen, there are thousands of such women as these all over the country. Do they tend to the world's advancement? Are they fit to rear intelligent citizens and to mold the characters of future generations that shall be an honor to our Republic?

These women in being deprived of the ballot are shut off from one of the greatest educational methods. If they were voters, their husbands would respect their opinions and instead of spending their time gaining outside constituents would be gaining constituents by their own firesides. Think not that this change would unsex women; there would have to be a new creation for the feminine to become masculine, for the mother to forget her offspring or turn a deaf ear to the supplications of the weak and helpless. Women's brains and characters can develop; their nature is unchangeable. Even the fiercest and most tumultuous surroundings never alter the innate gentleness of certain men. Days of desperate carnage never made Stonewall Jackson forget his highest duty, as leaning on his musket in the starlit night he held communion with his God. A hundred battlefields never hardened General Lee, as with a heart pierced by a thousand sorrows he surrendered the sword of the lost cause at Appomattox. Such men as these never lose the innocence and gentleness with which they lisped their prayers at their mother's knees; neither can political affairs make women false to their inborn instincts or lose one atom of the soft, loving tenderness that God has implanted in their breasts.

When women's opinions are counted as well as men's, it will only be adding fresh dignity and respect to the home; it will only be opening the darkened windows and letting the sunshine of enlightenment nurture the nurseries of our nation. Voting will never lessen maternal love. Office holding will never smother conjugal affection. The hardest problems of government will never shatter love's young dream.

Gentlemen, in the name of these women of my State, and for the betterment of the wives, mothers, and daughters of our land, I implore you to use your influence for our enfranchisement.

Remarks of Orra Langhorne, of Virginia.

Mr. CHAIRMAN AND GENTLEMEN: As a citizen, a native, and a resident of Virginia, I am here this morning representing a number of Virginia women, to request that when the sixteenth amendment is reported from the Judiciary Committee, you will do all in your power to secure its passage.

While we acknowledge courtesy and chivalry on the part of the men of Virginia, yet they still demand of us money for taxes without giving us the corresponding representation. They refuse us admittance to, and the benefit of, the highest and best institutions of our State, which are supported by State funds. They hold us amenable to the laws which we have no voice in making; they still deny us the advantage of earning a living in the higher professions, and deny us admittance to the learned professions even after we have been allowed to fit ourselves in spite of great obstacles for earning a living in that way. Therefore we request that the ballot be given us in order that we may protect our interests as American citizens; and we believe it will be greatly to the advantage of the administration of public affairs in our own State, and we are determined that it shall be given to us.

Remarks of Virginia D. Young, of South Carolina.

GENTLEMEN: As a native and lifelong resident of South Carolina, I claim to represent her, and wish to call your attention to certain conditions in my State which imperatively demand for their amelioration and care the ballot in the hands of her women.

In the late constitutional convention it was admitted that we suffered frauds in our elections, and the committee on suffrage worked hard, devoting all its energies to concoct some plan by which white supremacy might be attained without trenching on the fifteenth amendment to the United States Constitution.

The plan finally resolved upon does not absolutely insure honest registering and honest elections. And therefore it has not solved the problem of giving a sense of protection and satisfaction to all our citizens. The truth is, the frauds that have prevailed in elections in my State constitute the taproot of lynchings and mob rule. Our negro population cherish a deep sense of being defrauded of their rights at the ballot box, and the sense of wrong among the more intelligent is communicated to the more brutal among them, and they, acting on the spur of deadly hatred, wreak their vengeance on the helpless and innocent. Rape and murder and house burning all recur again and again, perpetrated by these ignorant people.

Gentlemen, give the women of South Carolina the ballot, with a property and educational qualification, and they will outnumber the negro voters so that these people's ballots can be honestly counted.

I believe from my heart that woman suffrage in South Carolina will settle straightway the present strained and uneasy relations between the races and stop the brutal crimes to punish which our impulsive white citizens take the law into their own hands and horrify the best people in our State, as well as the outside world, by lynching.

6-b

"Do a Majority of Women... Want the Ballot?"

Antisuffragists also used the opportunity provided by congressional committees to present their arguments and spread their propaganda. The statement of one Franklin W. Collins of Nebraska before the Senate Woman Suffrage Committee in April, 1912, is a typical example of antisuffrage arguments.

Document†

Statement of Mr. Franklin W. Collins, of Nebraska.

Mr. COLLINS. Mr. Chairman and members of the honorable committee, I am opposed to the proposed amendment to the Constitution granting the privileges and burdens of the franchise to women, and, with your indulgence, shall outline my objections to the same in a series of questions, intelligent and candid answer to which would seem to dispose of the plea which has been made for this so-called relief.

Why an amendment to the Constitution of the United States, and the preliminary steps leading thereto, when the States possess the power to extend the suffrage to women if they will?

Do a majority of the women of the United States want the ballot?

If not, and it is no where seriously contended that they do, should it be forced upon the majority by the minority?

Would it benefit womankind to have it?

Would it be wise to thrust the ballot upon those who do not seek it or want it?

Would it benefit the country?

Is it not incumbent upon its advocates to show that it would be beneficial to womankind or country, if not both?

Are there not too many stay-at-homes among the voters as it is?

†From: U.S., Congress, Senate, Committee on Woman Suffrage, 62nd Cong., 2d sess., Document no. 601, pp. 26-31.

After the novelty has worn away, and the privilege of voting becomes irksome, would not women be liable to stay at home in large and ever increasing numbers?

Is not this the experience of those States and communities where the experiment has been tried?

Is it not a fact that the persons we least like to see vote are the ones who invariably vote, and those we most desire to vote are the persons who often refrain from voting? Will this be changed when women secure the ballot?

Is not the influence of woman to-day greater without the ballot than it would or could be with it?

Is she not the life and hope of the home, the church, of charity work, and society, and are not her hands full to overflowing already?

In other words, is not the average good woman at the present time carrying all the burdens which she has the time and strength to carry?

Can she add to her responsibilities without materially substracting from her efficiency in the home, the church, and society?

Is not her influence as a home-maker and a home-keeper far more helpful to humanity than it would be were she given the ballot, together with its accompaniments?

If she accepts a portion of the responsibility has she any right to balk at the acceptance of the whole? Is not this unequal suffrage?

Is it not "a sin against abstract justice" to take the ballot and decline to accept the responsibilities which are its inevitable accompaniments?

Is this in accord with the doctrine of "a square deal"?

Are the women of the Nation willing to accept it on such terms?

If, by her ballot, she should plunge the country into war, would she not be in honor bound to fight by the side of man—to accept the consequences of her own exercise of political power?

If not, why not? Is not power without responsibility tyranny?

Would not her embarkation upon the troubled sea of politics weaken her present position and influence in the home, the church, and society?

Does not experience teach that the good women of the country, if united, can secure anything within reason which they want without the ballot?

What substantial advantage, then, can they hope to gain by the use of the ballot?

Are not the rights of women protected and safeguarded under the present system?

If any evils there be, which are curable by legislation, and the women of the land unite to demand their correction, does not the experience of the past warrant the assertion and conclusion that they would be more speedily righted without the ballot than with it?

Statement has been made at the present hearing that, in the factories, women are discriminated against by reason of their sex, and that the wages paid to men are nearly twice as high as those paid to women. Is not this statement grossly inaccurate? After a most painstaking and complete investigation, covering many years and embracing all the factories of the country, made, too, in large part, to determine as to whether discrimination of the kind complained of existed, the Bureau of Labor of the United States declares most positively that the charges made are utterly unfounded, and that women for the same work receive the same wages as men. Which statement is entitled to the greater weight, that of the petitioners or that of the Bureau of Labor?

What is there to indicate that women would vote as a substantial unit on any great moral issue?

"Wisdom is justified by its fruits." Have women, when given the ballot, shown by their fruits that it has been of positive advantage to community, Commonwealth, country, or to themselves?

Judged by its fruits, has the experiment of equal suffrage proven a success in Colorado, Wyoming, or elsewhere?

Is it not unsatisfactory, particularly as tried and applied in large cities?

Is not the government of our large cities one of the very gravest, if not the gravest, of our problems?

Is not the enfranchisement of women likely to add to the seriousness of the problem, rather than take therefrom?

Is not Denver, despite the ballot in the hands of women, as badly governed as before?

Would equal suffrage accomplish for New York, Philadelphia, Boston, Chicago, Pittsburgh, and St. Louis what it has failed to do for Denver, to wit, clean the Augean stables?

Has the granting of the ballot to the women of Colorado, Wyoming, Utah, Idaho (California being in her swaddling clothes as yet, speaking suffragetically), purified politics, uprooted fraud and corruption, or resulted in the enactment of reformatory legislation in behalf of the home or the children of the home?

One of the most effective arguments used by the advocates of female suffrage to induce the support of many women is that it will place in the hands of women the instrument with which to grind the traffic in alcoholic stimulants to powder, and that once given this opportunity, they will wipe the business of liquor selling off the map of America. After saying as they do that the abolition of this evil or its effective regulation is a total failure in the hands of man, the question is pertinent, Have the women kept their promise in this respect in a single State or community wherein they have been clothed with the suffrage? If so, would not Colorado, Wyoming, Utah, and Idaho be prohibition States?

On the other hand, is it not true that in every instance in which a State or a community have banished the traffic in alcoholic stimulants the ballot has been in the hands of male voters alone?

But should it be admitted that the ballot in the hands of women has been successful in some of our Western Commonwealths, where the men largely outnumber the women, and where the percentage of illiteracy is almost nothing, and where the people are widely scattered, and the population composed almost entirely of native Americans, the foreign born among them being of the better types in the main—hardy, self-reliant, accustomed to the wind and the rain and the sun—does it follow that the experiment would work to advantage in our Eastern States (not to speak of our Southern States, with their black belt), running over as they are with swarms of ignorant and degraded people living in the slums of our great cities—vast swarms of both sexes, appallingly vicious?

Have the women who would secure this privilege counted the cost of adding not alone the vote of the good and the cultured women to the electorate, but that of the illiterate, the ignorant, and the bad?

Even if it were susceptible of positive proof that women in the mass are more intelligent than men in the mass, nevertheless should women demand the ballot unless and until she has at least convinced herself, if not others, that the things to be gained thereby are of greater value than the things to be lost in the operation?

Have the women of the United States who are waging this campaign for the ballot weighed the possible loss as against the possible gain?

May we not answer the oft appealed to aphorism that "it is absurd to call those free who have no voice in framing the laws they are forced to obey," by inquiring if woman does not indeed and in truth have a mighty strong voice in framing the laws, if only she sees fit to exert it, and that her voice is none the less felt and followed, because she does not go to the polls or sit in the Halls of Congress?

Show me a Congress or a State legislature which would dare to overlook the wish and the will of womankind when once made known. Much has been said about the suffrage being a natural right, as, for instance, "Life, liberty, and the pursuit of happiness." Is the suffrage such a right?

Is it not both a privilege and a burden imposed by the sovereignty, which is the Government of the United States, under its Constitution, upon certain of the people of the country, who possess the qualifications fixed by that Constitution, and only upon those who measure up to such requirements?

If a natural or absolute right, to which all persons without regard to race or sex or color or what not are entitled to have and hold and exercise without question, why do we deprive our men of it until they arrive at the age of 21 years, why is it this so-called right is denied to the people of the Territories and the people of the District of Columbia?

If an absolute right, by what authority or color of authority does the State of Massachusetts, as well as other States, bar from the use and enjoyment of the suffrage men who do not possess certain prescribed educational qualifications?

Is it not true that every free lover, every socialist, every communist, and every anarchist the country over is openly in favor of female suffrage?

Does not the ballot in the hands of woman seem to give aid and comfort to schemes to overthrow the family and the private home?

Is not one of the saddest problems which the country faces to-day the disintegration of the American home?

Are not too many homes torn with discord and dissension, are not the divorce courts strewn with family skeletons, thick as leaves in the forests of Valambrosa?

Will the ballot in the hands of women pour oil on the troubled domestic waters?

Will not its inevitable tendency be to furnish still another cause of friction and irritation?

Speaking very seriously, and not wishing to be thought guilty of indelicacy, is it not a fact requiring no argument to support it that woman by her very organism and temperament—so fundamentally different and so delicate as compared with man—is not fitted to blaze man's trail or do man's work in the world any more than man is fitted to fill woman's sacred place and do her work in the world?

In other words, is not the so-called reform sought a reform against nature, unscientific and unsound?

Much has been said about the emancipation of woman, as if she were held in bondage through the tyranny of man or government. Are not the women of America the freest beings of their sex on the planet, and fully able to secure any of their sovereign rights, or redress any and all of their wrongs, if they will only unite and make their wants known—that is to say, if remedy by legislative action is possible?

To the statement that men have made a mess of government and women could hardly do any worse, is it not sufficient to ask the gentler sex if she has proven "by her fruits," when put to the solemn test, that she could reduce the chaos to cosmos?

There is a growing and a distinctly alarming tendency in this country on the part of women to escape the so-called drudgery of housekeeping, and particularly the burdens of child-bearing and child-rearing, so that we find many of those who are best equipped for wifehood and motherhood refusing to listen to its sacred call, while those who are illy equipped for it answering the same call unquestioningly.

Do you not think this movement has a strong tendency to encourage this exodus from "the land of bondage," otherwise known as matrimony and motherhood?

While this honorable committee is assembled here to consider the conferring of the suffrage upon woman thousands of the bonniest youths and fairest maidens of America are taking the first downward step. In a little while they will be going at a cataract pace. Would it not seem that the same energy, determination, and rare ability displayed by the advocates of this privilege and burden, of doubtful value, could be more worthily bestowed in saving the boys and girls of the land from irretrievable disaster, which, of course, means inevitably the shipwreck of country and civilization?

Is not the need of the land and the age a return to the old-fashioned, cardinal, and never-to-be-improved-upon virtues—a return to the first principles of right thinking and right living—a renaissance of the American family, which is fast being deserted by its former devotees; to speak plainly, that woman shall not flee from her high and holy mission as though it were a plague, so that no longer the finest product of America—the children—shall, in case they are permitted to arrive at all, be turned over to the tender mercies of hirelings for their training and mothering, or be allowed to bring themselves up with the chances that in the end away they will go to perdition, across lots; but instead of that they shall be trained in their own homes by their own mothers (I never knew a father who amounted to very much in this line, though he should boost all he can in the right direction); trained in the way they should go, in the full assurance of Holy Writ that when they are old they will not depart therefrom.

Finally, gentlemen, can the good women of the land help themselves, their country, or humanity, now or hereafter, in a more effective way than by the organization of a nation-wide back-to-home movement?

Do not the present propaganda and program mean a long step in the backward direction?

Is it not emphatically a movement away from home, away from nature, and away from those exalted ideals following which man and woman have struggled upward together from the depths of barbarism to the loftiest plane of civilization and progress the world has ever known?

I thank you.

7-a

Carrie Chapman Catt Describes the Opposition

In 1915 Carrie Chapman Catt told a Senate committee how the women of New York had organized for their suffrage referendum, and how—in her view—they came to be outvoted, even though they had turned out a half-million votes for suffrage.

Document†

In contrast we may ask what have women done? Again I may say that New York is a fair example because it is the largest of the States in population and has the second city in size in the world and occupies perhaps the most important position in any land in which a suffrage referendum has been taken. Women held during the six months prior to the election in 1915, 10,300 meetings. They printed and circulated 7,500,000 leaflets or three-and-a-half for every voter. These leaflets weighed more than twenty tons. They had 770 treasuries in the State among the different groups doing suffrage work and every bookkeeper except two was a volunteer. Women by the thousands contributed to the funds of that campaign, in one group 12,000 public school teachers. On election day 6,330 women watched at the polls from 5:45 in the morning until after the vote was counted. I was on duty myself from 5:30 until midnight. There were 2,500 campaign officers in the State who gave their time without pay. The publicity features were more numerous and unique than any campaign of men or women had ever had. They culminated in a parade in New York City which was organized without any effort to secure women outside the city to participate in it, yet 20,000 marched through Fifth Avenue to give some idea of the size of their demand for the vote.

What was the result? If we take the last announcement from the board of elections the suffrage amendment received 535,000 votes—2,000 more than the total vote of the nine States where women now have suffrage through a referendum. It was not submitted in Wyoming, Utah or Illinois. Yet New York suffragists did not win because the opponents outvoted them. How did

†From: Ida Husted Harper, ed. *History of Woman Suffrage,* (New York: J. J. Little and Ives, 1922. Vol. V, p. 753.

this happen? Why did not such evidence of a demand win the vote? Because the unscrupulous men of the State worked and voted against woman suffrage, aided and abetted by the weakminded and illiterate, who are permitted a vote in New York. In Rochester the male inmates of the almshouse and rescue home were taken out to vote against the amendment. Men too drunk to sign their own names voted all over the State, for drunkards may vote in New York. In many of the polling places the women watchers reported that throughout the entire day not one came to vote who did not have to be assisted; they did not know enough to cast their own vote.

"Merely to Stay in the Home is not Enough…"

After 1900 suffragists increasingly reached out in search of support from people who had not hitherto showed much interest in the movement. In the pamphlet reprinted below, Susan Walker Fitzgerald, a Bryn Mawr graduate and social worker, and veteran of outdoor campaigns in Massachusetts, appealed to women on the basis of their love of home and children. The pamphlet was designed to be read quickly and easily.

Document†

Women In The Home

By SUSAN W. FITZGERALD

We are forever being told that the place of woman is in the HOME. Well, so be it. But what do we expect of her in the home? Merely to stay in the home is not enough. She is a failure unless she does certain things for the home. She must make the home minster, as far as her means allow, to the health and welfare, moral as well as physical, of her family, and especially of her children. She, more than anyone else, is held responsible for what they become.

SHE is responsible for the cleanliness of her house.

SHE is responsible for the wholesomeness of the food.

SHE is responsible for the children's health.

SHE, above all, is responsible for their morals, for their sense of truth, of honesty and of decency, for what they turn out to be.

How Far Can the Mother Control These Things? She can clean her own rooms, BUT if the neighbors are allowed to live in filth, she cannot keep her rooms from being filled with bad airs and smells, or from being infested by vermin.

She can cook her food well, BUT if dealers are permitted to sell poor food, unclean milk or stale eggs, she cannot make the food wholesome for her children.

She can care for her own plumbing and her refuse, BUT if the plumbing in the rest of the house is unsanitary, if garbage accumulates and the halls and

†From: *Political Equality*, leaflet published by the National American Woman Suffrage Association.

114

stairs are left dirty, she cannot protect her children from the sickness and infection that these conditions bring.

She can take every care to avoid fire, BUT if the house has been badly built, if the fire-escapes are insufficient or not fire-proof, she cannot guard her children from the horrors of being maimed or killed by fire.

She can open her windows to give her children the air that we are told is so necessary, BUT if the air is laden with infection, with tuberculosis and other contagious diseases, she cannot protect her children from this danger.

She can send her children out for air and exercise, BUT if the conditions that surround them on the streets are immoral and degrading, she cannot protect them from these dangers.

ALONE, she CANNOT make these things right. WHO or WHAT can?

THE CITY can do it, the CITY GOVERNMENT that is elected BY THE PEOPLE, to take care of the interests of THE PEOPLE.

And who decides what the city government shall do?

FIRST, the officials of that government; and,

SECOND, those who elect them.

DO THE WOMEN ELECT THEM? NO, the men do. So it is the MEN and NOT THE WOMEN that are really responsible for the unclean houses, unwholesome food, bad plumbing, danger of fire, risk of tuberculosis and other diseases, immoral influences of the street. In fact, MEN are responsible for the conditions under which the children live, but we hold WOMEN responsible for the results of those conditions. If we hold women responsible for the results, must we not, in simple justice, let them have something to say as to what these conditions shall be? There is one simple way of doing this. Give them the same means that men have, LET THEM VOTE.

Women are by nature and training, housekeepers, Let them have a hand in the city's housekeeping, even if they introduce an occasional house-cleaning.

7-C

The Illinois Suffrage Campaign

Energy, new members, and the effective organizational techniques made possible the adoption of suffrage amendments in a number of western states after 1910. In 1913, a lucky political situation gave the Progressives in Illinois the balance of power in the legislature, and their leader, Medill McCormick, was a strong suffragist. The women in the Equal Suffrage League were well-organized, and ready to go. Together they concentrated on a bill based on the constitutional provision that state legislatures could set the qualifications for federal electors. In 1920 Grace Wilbur Trout (who had been president of the suffrage association) set down the story of how that campaign was won.

Document†

The Presidential and Municipal Suffrage Bill was introduced in the House by Representative Charles L. Scott (Dem.) and in the Senate by Senator Hugh S. Magill (Rep.). It was decided however, to let the suffrage bill lie quiescent in the House and secure its passage first through the Senate.

After nearly three months of strenuous effort the bill finally passed the Senate on May 7th by a vote of 29 yeas (3 more than the required majority) to 15 nays. . . .

The day the bill passed the Senate I left Springfield immediately to address a suffrage meeting to be held in Galesburg that evening, and the next day went to Monmouth where another meeting was held. In both of these towns there was a member of the House who was marked on the card index as "doubtful." Both of these Legislators however, afterwards, through the influence of their respective constituents voted for the suffrage measure. We soon discovered that there was no class of people for whom a politician had so tender and respectful a regard as for his voting constituents.

After I left Springfield that week Mrs. Booth remained to see that the Suffrage Measure got safely over to the House. In the meantime there was a mix-up and the suffrage bill was taken by mistake directly to the Committee on Elections without first being recommended to that Committee by the Speaker of the House. There was an immediate outcry on the part of the opponents of the measure at such irregular procedure. It was very amusing to

†From: Grace Wilbur Trout, "Sidelights on Illinois Suffrage History," *Journal of the Illinois State Historical Society* 12, no. 2 (July 1920): 145-79.

find that other Senate bills had been put through in this way and no objections had been raised, but it aroused fierce indignation with the suffrage bill, for the men at Springfield said there had never been such opposition to any other bill.

When I returned to Springfield the following week after this mistake had been made, I learned a lesson about the inadvisability of talking on elevators. I was on an elevator at the Capitol when some of our legislative opponents, who were in a facetious mood, got on, and one of them remarked, with a sidelong glance at me, "How surprised some folks will be later on," and laughed so jubilantly as I got off the elevator that it made me thoughtful. After some meditation I decided that there was an intention to put the suffrage bill into the wrong Committee, and this surmise was afterwards proven correct. We wished it to go into the Elections Committee, where we had already ascertained we had sufficient votes to get it out with a favorable recommendation, however, if it was ordered into the Judiciary Committee, it would fall into the hands of the enemy and be killed forever. We worked into the small hours of the night carefully making our plans for the next day. In the meantime James A. Watson, one of our faithful friends and Chairman of the Elections Committee, had returned the suffrage bill to Speaker McKinley, and arrangements were made so that the Speaker could properly turn it over to the Elections Committee. When the morning session opened the bill was ordered to the Elections Committee before our opponents realized their little plot had been frustrated. We were not surprised, but they were.

It is doubtful whether we could have secured this favorable action without the powerful assistance of David E. Shanahan. The latter on account of being from a foreign district in Chicago, felt he could not vote for the suffrage bill, but he gave us the benefit of his wise counsel. In fact to overcome the pitfalls, which surround the passage of every bill upon which there is a violent difference of opinion, I appealed to the enemies of the measure to give the women of Illinois a square deal. On account of his great influence with other members I especially appealed to Mr. Lee O'Neil Browne, a powerful Democratic leader and one of the best parliamentarians in the House. Mr. Browne had always opposed suffrage legislation but he finally consented to let the bill, so far as he was concerned, come up to Third Reading, so that it could come out in the open and be voted up or down on its merits, stating frankly that he would try to defeat the bill on the floor of the House. It was this spirit of fair play among the opponents of the measure as well as the loyalty of its friends, that afterwards made possible the great victory of 1913.

During this time Mrs. Booth and I worked alone at Springfield, but now we sent for Mrs. Antoinette Funk of Chicago, who had been an active worker in the Progressive Party, to come to Springfield and she arrived on May 13th. Mrs. Funk was a lawyer, and her legal experience made her services at this time very valuable. A week later, on May 20th, Mrs. Medill McCormick, with her new baby girl, moved from Chicago to Springfield and we immediately enlisted her services. Mrs. McCormick, as the daughter of the late Mark

Hanna, had inherited much of her father's keen interest in politics and she was a welcome and most valuable addition to our forces.

The suffrage bill was called up for Second Reading on June 3rd. There was a most desperate attempt at this time to amend, and if possible kill the measure, but it finally passed on to Third Reading without any changes—just as it had come over from the Senate. During this period we found that we were being shadowed by detectives, and we were on our guard constantly and never talked over any plans when we were in any public place.

The hope of the opposition now was to influence Speaker McKinley and prevent the bill from coming up, and let it die, as so many bills do die, on Third Reading. Sometimes bills come up that many Legislators do not favor but to preserve their good records they feel obliged to vote for, then afterwards these Legislators appeal to the Speaker of the House and ask him to save them by preventing it from ever coming to a final vote. If he is adroit, this can be done without the people as a whole knowing what has happened to some of their favorite measures. Mr. Edward D. Shurtleff said this was done session after session when he was Speaker of the House by the men who had promised to vote for the suffrage bill but never wanted it under any circumstances to pass. The young Speaker of the House looked worn and haggard during these trying days—he told me he had not been allowed to sleep for many nights—that hundreds of men from Chicago and from other parts of Illinois had come down and begged him to never let the suffrage bill come up for the final vote, and threatened him with political oblivion if he did. He implored me to let him know if there was any suffrage sentiment in Illinois.

I immediately telephoned to Chicago to Margaret Dobyne, our faithful Press Chairman, to send the call out for help all over the State, asking for telegrams and letters to be sent at once to Speaker McKinley asking him to bring up the suffrage measure and have it voted upon. She called in Jennie F.W. Johnson, the State Treasurer, Mrs. J.W. McGraw, and other members of the Board and secured the assistance of Mrs. Judith W. Loewenthal, Mrs. Charles L. Nagely, Mrs. L. Brackett Bishop and other active suffragists to help in this work, and wherever possible they reached nearby towns by telephone.

In the meantime I also phoned Mrs. Harriette Taylor Treadwell, President of the Chicago Political Equality League, to have Speaker McKinley called up by phone and interviewed when he returned to Chicago that week, and to also have letters and telegrams waiting for him when he returned to Springfield. She organized the novel, and now famous, telephone brigade, by means of which Speaker McKinley was called up every 15 minutes by leading men as well as women, both at his home and at his office from early Saturday morning until Monday evening, the days he spent in Chicago. His mother, whom we entertained at a luncheon after the bill had passed, said that it was simply one continuous ring at their house and that someone had to sit right by the phone to answer the calls. Mrs. Treadwell was ably assisted in this work by Mrs. James W. Morrison, President of the Chicago Equal Suffrage Association, Mrs. Jeane Wallace Butler, a well known manufacturer and exporter, who appealed to business women, Mrs. Edward L. Stillman, an active suffragist in the Rogers Park Woman's Club, Miss Florence King, President of the Woman's Association of Commerce, Miss Mary Miller, President of Chicago Human Rights Association, Mrs. Charlotte Rhodus, President of the Woman's Party of Cook County, Miss Belle Squire, President of the No-Vote No-Tax League, and others.

When the Speaker reached Springfield Tuesday morning there were thousands of letters and telegrams waiting for him from every section of Illinois. He needed no further proof that there was suffrage sentiment in Illinois, and acted accordingly. He announced that the suffrage bill would be brought up for the final vote on June 11th. We immediately got busy. We divided up our friends among the Legislators and each man was personally interviewed by either Mrs. Booth, Mrs. Funk, Mrs. McCormick, or myself.

As soon as the bill had passed the Senate we had realized that with 153 members in the House, we would need help in rounding up the "votes," so we immediately selected sixteen House members whom we appointed as Captains, each Captain was given so many men to look after and see that these men were in their seats whenever the suffrage bill came up for consideration.

The latter part of the week before the bill was to be voted upon I sent telegrams to every man who had promised to vote for the bill in the House, asking him to be present if possible on Tuesday morning as the suffrage bill was to be voted upon Wednesday, June 11th, and we would feel safer to have our friends on hand early.

When the morning of June 11th came there was suppressed excitement at the Capitol. The Captains previously requested to be on hand were there rounding up their men and reporting if any were missing. We immediately called up those who were not there, and if necessary, sent a cab after them, which we had engaged for the day to be ready for any emergency. There was one young man who was especially efficient in the telephone booth so we engaged him to stay at his post all day, so that we could secure quick telephone service when needed.

We all wanted to be in the gallery where we could see that last dramatic struggle, but it seemed to me wiser to have the entrance of the House guarded to prevent any friendly Legislators from leaving during roll call, and to prevent any of our opponents from violating the law and entering the House during the session. The husky door-keeper, who was opposed to suffrage, could not be counted upon to keep out anti-suffrage lobbyists if they desired to enter, consequently I took up my post near the House door, which was the only entrance left open that day, and was furnished a chair by the man who conducted a cigar stand near the entrance. Mrs. Booth and Mrs. McCormick sat in the gallery and checked off the votes, and Mrs. Funk carried messages and instructions and kept me advised of the developments in the House. Shortly after the session opened the before mentioned door-keeper came and very brusquely ordered me to go to the gallery. Around the rotunda rail lounged a number of our opponents, so I said I preferred to remain where I was. He scowled his disapproval, and presently returned and said that one of the House members who was an active opponent of our measure, said if I did not go to the gallery at once he would introduce and pass a resolution forcing me to do so. I answered politely saying that of course the member was privileged to introduce any resolution he desired, but in the meantime I would remain where I was. The men around the rotunda rail were watching the whole procedure and when I still remained in spite of this warning they regarded me with unfriendly eyes. There was a lawyer among them who longed to get inside that day, but he did not like, even with the backing of a friendly door-keeper, to violate the law—that forbade any lobbyist to enter the House after the session had convened—in my presence. The door-keeper in reporting the incident afterwards said "I did not dare touch her and march her up into the gallery where she belonged." As a matter of fact any citizen of Illinois had a legal right to be where I was, if he so desired. In the meantime several friends becoming tired with the long discussions and frequent roll calls, started to leave, but I persuaded them in the interest of a great cause, to return. So while I could only hear the sound of voices and from Mrs. Funk's reports get some idea of the fight that was raging inside, I was glad that I had remained as guardian of the door, for the main all-important object after all was to pass the bill.

During this time a House member came rushing out and said "We have lost." I immediately sent the boy, whom we had engaged for this purpose, for Mrs. Funk and told her I knew there was a mistake for we had the votes and no men had left the House. Shortly afterwards there was a deafening roar and several men rushed out and exclaimed "We have won. The bill has passed." I remember of turning my face to the wall and shedding a few quiet tears and when I looked around there were about ten men who were all surreptitiously wiping their eyes. The Presidential and Municipal Suffrage Bill passed the House by the following vote: Yeas 83 (6 more than the required majority) to Nays 58.

It was a great victory. It was claimed there was plenty of money at Springfield—a million dollars or more—ready to be used to defeat the law, but not one Illinois Legislator could be influenced to break his word. The bill was passed through the co-operation and voting together of men from all political parties, men of different religious faiths, and it was dramatic on the floor of the House to have the fight for our bill led by Edward D. Shurtleff, at that time leader of the "wets" and George H. Wilson, leader of the "drys." It was clearly demonstrated that we may as a people, differ on questions of creed, and honestly differ on questions of policy—these differences of opinion are after all, purely matters of birth and environment—but there are great fundamental principles of right which touch human happiness and human life upon which we all stand together.

In fact the men who voted for the suffrage bill at Springfield had become convinced that the suffrage bill was basic in its nature and stood back of, and took precedence over all other measures for philanthropy and reform. They realized also that no state would even be approaching permanent better conditions with a fundamental wrong at the core of its Government, and that "in a Governmen of the people, by the people, and for the people"— "people" could be interpreted only as meaning women as well as men.

The Illinois Legislators in voting for the suffrage measure made themselves forever great—they gave Illinois a place in history no other State can ever fill, for Illinois was the first State east of the Mississippi and the first State even bordering the great father of waters, to break down the conservatism of the great Middle West and give suffrage to its women. It was claimed that there had been no event since the Civil War of such far reaching national significance as the passage of the suffrage bill in Illinois. This seemed like a prophecy, for since that time Mrs. Carrie Chapman Catt, President of the National American Woman Suffrage Association, said that New York women never could have won their great suffrage victory in 1917 if Illinois had not first opened the door in 1913, and the winning of suffrage in New York so added to the political strength of the suffrage movement in Congress that it made possible the passage of the Federal Suffrage Amendment in 1919, so the work in Illinois was fundamental and as vitally important to the women of the whole nation as it was to the women of Illinois.

. . . .

As there had been no time during this strenuous period to raise funds, when we returned to Chicago we found the State Treasury empty although the entire cost of the Springfield campaign, which lasted for over six months and included railroad fare for the lobbyists to and from Springfield, innumerable telegrams, and long distance telephone calls, postage, stationery, printing, stenographic help, hotel bills and incidentals, was only $1,567.26. We therefore very gratefully accepted the offer of the Chicago Examiner to publish a suffrage edition of that paper, and netted as a result, about $15,000, for the suffrage cause. . . .

7-d

"On Behalf of 7,000,000 Wage-Earning Women..."

After 1900 more and more suffragists tried to cross class lines and bring middle class and working women together in their fight for the right to vote. At a hearing on April 23, 1912 before a joint committee drawn from the Judiciary Committee and the Woman Suffrage Committee of the Senate one of the speakers identified herself as spokesmen for wage-earners, and another spoke as one who had been a wage-earner since the age of thirteen.

Document†

Statement of Miss Caroline A. Lowe, of Kansas City, Mo.

Miss LOWE. Gentlemen of the committee, it is as a wage earner and on behalf of the 7,000,000 wage-earning women in the United States that I wish to speak.

I entered the ranks of the wage earners when 18 years of age. Since then I have earned every cent of the cost of my own maintenance, and for several years was a potent factor in the support of my widowed mother.

Need of the Ballot. The need of the ballot for the wage-earning women is a vital one. No plea can be made that we have the protection of the home or are represented by our fathers or brothers. We need the ballot that we may broaden our horizon and assume our share in the solution of the problems that seriously affect our daily lives. There is no question that the exercise of the right to vote on matters of public concern enlarges the sense of public responsibility. While in Colorado, visiting a friend who had formerly been a teacher in Kansas, she assured me that the average woman teacher in Colorado, where the women have the full right of franchise, is as fully informed on all political matters as is the average man teacher in Kansas, while the average woman teacher in Kansas ranks below the man in this respect.

We need the ballot for the purpose of self-protection. Last Saturday afternoon, at the closing hour at Marshall Field's in Chicago, a young woman

†From: U.S., Congress, Senate, Joint Committee, 62nd Cong., 2nd sess., S. Document 601, pp. 16-20.

cashier fell on the floor in a dead faint and was carried away by her fellow workers. Long hours of the rush and strain of the Saturday shopping had overcome her. The 10-hour law is not a 10-hour law for us. We must be up at 6 in order to be at work by 8. It requires two hours after work for us to reach home and eat our evening meal. Fourteen hours out of the twenty-four are consumed entirely by our daily efforts to make a living. If we secure any education or amusement it leaves us but seven or eight hours for sleep, and this generally in insanitary and unwholesome surroundings.

Does the young woman cashier in Marshall Field's need any voice in making the law that sets the hours of labor that shall constitute a day's work?

In the Boston Store, at the same hour, a delicate slip of a girl employed as an inspector was on the verge of a hysterical breakdown. The floor woman, in all kindness, said to her: "My dear, it is useless to feel like this now. The busy season is just beginning, and you will have to stand it." Receiving a wage of $4.50 a week, has this girl any need of a voice in demanding a minimum-wage law?

Has the young woman whose scalp was torn from her head at the Lawrence mill any need of a law demanding that safety appliances be placed upon all dangerous machinery?

And what of the working girls who, through unemployment, are denied the opportunity to sell the labor of their hands and are driven to the sale of their virtue?

I met Katie Malloy under peculiar circumstances. It was because of this that she told me of her terrible struggles during the great garment-workers' strike in Chicago. She had worked at Hart, Schaffner & Marx's for five years, and had saved $30 out of her wages. It was soon gone. She hunted for work, applied at the Young Women's Christian Association and was told that so many hundreds of girls were out of work that they could not possibly do anything for her. She walked the streets day after day without success. For three days she had almost nothing to eat. "Oh," she said, with tears streaming down her cheeks, "there is always some place where a man can crowd in and keep decent, but for us girls there is no place—no place but one, and it is thrown open to us day and night. Hundreds of girls that worked by me in the shop have gone into houses of—houses of impurity."

Has Katie Malloy and the 5,000 working girls who are forced into lives of shame each month no need of a voice in a government that should protect them from this life which is worse than death?

The Working Woman and the Workingman. From the standpoint of wages received we wage earners know it to be almost universal that the men in the industries receive twice the wage granted to us, although we may be doing the same work and should have the same pay. We women work side by side with our brothers. We are children of the same parents, reared in the same homes, educated in the same schools, ride to and fro on the same early morning and late evening cars, work together the same number of hours in the same shops, and we have equal need of food, clothing, and shelter. But at 21 years of age our brothers are given a powerful weapon for self-defense, a larger means for growth and self-expression.

We working women, even because we are women and find our sex not a source of strength, but a source of weakness and offering a greater opportunity for exploitation, are denied this weapon.

Gentlemen of the committee, is there any justice underlying such a condition? If our brother workingmen are granted the ballot with which to protect themselves, do you not think that the working women should be granted this same right?

The Working Girl Vs. Her Employer. What of the working girl and her employer? Why is the ballot given to him while it is denied to us? Is it for the protection of his property, that he may have a voice in the governing of his wealth, of his stocks and bonds and merchandise?

The wealth of the working woman is of far greater value to the State. From nature's raw products the working class can readily replace all of the material wealth owned by the employing class, but the wealth of the working woman is the wealth of flesh and blood, of all her physical, mental, and spiritual powers. It is the wealth, not only of to-day, but that of future generations, that is being bartered away so cheaply. Have we no right to a voice in the disposal of our wealth, the greatest wealth that the world possesses—the priceless wealth of its womanhood?

Is it not the cruelest injustice that the man whose material wealth is a source of strength and protection to him and of power over us should be given the additional advantage of an even greater weapon which he can use to perpetuate our condition of helpless subjection?

Discrimination Against Disfranchised Class. You say the ballot is not a factor as a means of discrimination between the workingman and the working woman. We found a most striking example of the falsity of this statement a few years ago in Chicago. The Chicago teachers, firemen, and policemen had had their salaries cut because of the poverty of the city. The teachers' salaries were cut the third time. They organized to investigate the reason for the reduction. Margaret Haley was selected to carry on the investigation. As a result, she unearthed large corporations that were not paying the legal amount of taxes. The teachers forced the issue, and as a result nearly $600,000 in taxes was annually forced from the corporations and turned into the public treasury. What was done with it? The policemen and firemen had the cut in their salaries restored, while the teachers did not. Instead, the finance committee recommended and the board of education appropriated the teachers' share to pay coal bills, repairs, etc. Why was this? It was a clear case of the usual treatment accorded to a disfranchised class.

Industrial Revolution Precedes Political Evolution. However, Mr. Chairman, as students of sociology we are forced to recognize the fact that the ballot has never yet been granted by a ruling class because of the needs of a serving class.

Almost without exception the extension of the franchise has taken place only when the needs of the industrial development have demanded a larger degree of freedom upon the part of the serving class, so that the serving class, driven by the very pressure of economic need, has organized as a class, and, after a struggle, has wrested from the grasp of the ruling class a larger share in the powers of government.

Instance after instance of the truth of this assertion presents itself. At the breaking up of the feudal system, the peasants, in large numbers, left the estates of their masters and entered upon the new form of industry made possible through manufacturing. To escape the robbery of the nobility, they organized in guilds. This organization was a necessity, not only for their protection, but also for the better development of their new form of industry. A larger freedom upon the part of the members of the guild was the inevitable outcome of the change in the industrial basis. As a result of the struggle, the members of the guilds forced the nobility to relinquish their exorbitant demands, and free towns came into existence. This increase in political liberty came as the direct result of the revolution that had taken place in the industrial life of a large number of the peasants of that day.

When the industrial basis of any society, or any portion of society, changes, the superstructure must change in accordance with it. This was again proved when the transition from the hand tool to machine production took place. Again it resulted in an extension of the franchise to a still larger portion of the working class.

Woman's Political Status Must Change to Conform With Change in Industrial Basis. It is this same revolution that has taken place in the life of the working woman. Within the last two generations the woman of the working class has been forced from her home into the industries.

The weaving that we used to do with our hand looms is now done in great factories requiring the services of hundreds of thousands of women and children. The meat that we used to cure in the smoke-house is now prepared in gigantic meat-packing establishments. Our butter is made at the creamery and our bread at the bakery. Even the education of our children is placed in the hands of the kindergarten and the public schools. There has been nothing for us to do but to follow our jobs into the great industrial centers.

History has proved that industrial revolutions are inevitably followed by political and social revolutions. The industrial basis of the life of the working woman has changed. The work that was formerly confined within the four walls of the home has gone to the centralized industries of the country, and the political superstructure must be adjusted to conform to this change. This industrial change has given to woman a larger horizon, a greater freedom of action in the industrial world. Greater freedom and larger expression are at hand for her in the political life.

Mr. Chairman and gentlemen of the committee, the time is ripe for the extension of the franchise to women. We do not come before you to beg you to grant us a favor; we come presenting to you a glorious opportunity to place yourselves abreast of the current of this great evolutionary movement. You can refuse to accept this opportunity, and you may, for a moment, delay the movement, but only as the old woman who, with her tiny broom, endeavored to sweep back the incoming tide from the sea.

If to-day, taking your places as men of affairs in the world's progress, you step out in unison with the eternal upward trend toward true democracy, you will support the suffrage amendment now before your committee. [Continued applause.]

Statement of Miss Leonora O'Reilly, of New York City.

Miss O'REILLY. Mr. Chairman and gentlemen of the committee: Yes; I have outdone the lady who went to work at 18 by five years. I have been a wage earner since I was a little over 13. I, too, know whereof I speak; that is the reason I do not want to play a bluff game with you any longer. You can not or will not make laws for us; we must make laws for ourselves. We working women need the ballot for self-protection; that is all there is to it. We have got to have it.

We work long, long hours and we do not get half enough to live on. We have got to keep decent, and if we go "the easy way" you men make the laws that will let you go free and send us into the gutter. [Applause.]

We can not believe in man-made laws any longer. We have gone from one assembly to another, from one State senator to another, and we have heard the same old story. You think only of output; there is not a soul among you who cares to save human beings. We have grown rich, as a nation, but we have grown very rotten. As a people—gentlemen, I use the term "rotten" advisedly—for, as far as the working women are concerned, the foundation we are building on is rotten. To purify the life of the Nation we women know we have got to do our part, political as well as industrial duty. Government, as a whole, rests on industry. You men say to us: "Go back to the home. Your place is in the home," yet as children we must come out of the home at 11, at 13, and at 15 years of age to earn a living; we have got to make good or starve.

"Pay your way" we are taught in school and in church—the greatest thing on earth is to be able to pay your way. Well, if any people on earth pay their way in life we working women do. The return we get is that most of us become physical wrecks along the roadside of life. When you gentlemen hear what it costs a working woman to "pay her way" in life, you sit back in your chairs, say "the story is terrible, but they manage to live somehow." Somehow—that is it, gentlemen. I want to make you realize the *somehow* of life to the hundreds of girls I have seen go down in the struggle. You men do not care. You want this country to get rich, and you do not know the only riches of a nation are its people. [Applause.]

We have gone before legislature after legislature making our pleas for justice. We have seen the game as you play it. What is it? We go there and we are told the same old tommyrot—let men do this for you. I tell you as a bit of business experience if you let anybody do a thing for you they will do you. That is business. [Applause.]

Now, while we have had the colleges opened to women, only one woman in a thousand goes to college, while modern industry claims one woman in every five to-day. It is industrial methods which are teaching the women the facts I am telling you. "Do the other fellow before he gets a chance to do you"—do him so hard that he can not stand up again; that is good business. We know that, and we women are sure that there must be some higher standard for life than business.

We are not getting a square deal; we go before legislature after legislature to tell our story, but they fail to help the women who are being speeded so high in the mills and in factories, from 54 hours to 72 hours in stores in New York, and 92 hours in one week in subcellar laundries. Who cares? Nobody! Nobody does; nobody cares about making laws so long as we get cheap and nasty things in the market. Working women come before you and tell you these things and think you will do something for them. Every man listening is convinced that the girls are telling the truth. It is only when you think of them as your own girls that you have the right to make laws for them. Every man listening wants to do the fair thing, but just as soon as our backs are turned, up comes the representative of the big interest and says, "Lad, you are dead politically if you do what those women ask." They know it is true, and we get nothing, because all the votes are owned.

Every vote you cast is owned, and it is the owned vote which has fought our women. Go before legislatures as you will, the only argument that you can bring in to the man in politics—he is there to go up the ladder, decently if he can, but he will go up anyhow, if he can—the only argument that you can bring to that man is the power of the ballot. When we can say to him. "Man, do this and we will return you so many million votes," he will listen and act.

This is what we want, because it is for the good of the women, because it is for the good of the whole people. It is for that reason that the working woman, facing the hard facts of life and having to fight her way, has come to the conclusion that you men in politics—I am not going to give you any taffy—you men in politics are not leaders, you follow what you think is the next step on the ladder. We want you to understand that the next step in politics, the next step in democracy, is to give to the women of your Nation a ballot. [Applause.]

The working women send me to you with the plain, honest truth; because, working beside you in the same mill or factory, we know you with your evening suit off and your tall hat in the box, or wherever it belongs; you are just a competitor with us there; we tell you the truth there, as I have come to tell you the truth here. Let women have the ballot, in order that you may once more throw the burden which you have carried, or thought you carried, onto them; that is the thing you have done since the beginning of time; when the load was too heavy for you you piled it onto Eve's back. [Applause.] You have got us in a devil of a mess, economic and political. It is so rank it smells to Heaven; but we will come in and help you clean house. We will start all over again, because we belong together shoulder to shoulder. We must get on to a better time. It is only because you will not, in your prejudice and your ignorance, let us into the political field with you that the situation is as bad as it is to-day.

We working women want the ballot, not as a privilege but as a right. You say you have only given the ballot as an expediency; you have never given it as a right; then we demand it as an expediency for the 8,000,000 working women. All other women ought to have it, but we working women must have it. [Applause.]

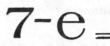

7-e

Mrs. Catt's Winning Plan

The turning point in the NAWSA campaign was often identified as the moment when Mrs. Catt at the emergency convention of 1916, unveiled her plan for a coordinated campaign, in which each state and local suffrage group would have its assigned task. Maud Wood Park, in her autobiographical account of the last phase of the suffrage battle, told how she perceived the sequence of events following upon the failure of both major political parties to adopt a strong federal suffrage plank.

Document†

That same afternoon Mrs. Catt, who was not in the habit of sitting down with a disappointment, held a meeting of the National Executive Board, which decided that, in view of the failure of both major parties to endorse the federal method of enfranchising women, an emergency convention of the whole Association ought to be called.

That convention met at Atlantic City in September to consider ways in which more effective action for the amendment might be taken. Both presidential candidates were invited to make addresses. Hon. Charles Evans Hughes, who was in the far West at the time, declined the invitation but issued a statement expressing approval of a federal woman suffrage amendment. President Wilson, who had previously advocated only the state-by-state method, came to Atlantic City and gave, in his speech there, the first public intimation that he would support the amendment.

"I have come to fight not for you but with you, and in the end I think we shall not quarrel over the method," was his assurance to the vast audience, listening as if life hung on his words.

At the close of the convention, Mrs. Catt called a session of the Executive Council, made up of the national officers of the Association and the presidents of its state branches. During the unusual heat of the preceding week she had conducted three meetings a day. She had borne, with no outward sign of disturbance, the responsibility of having the President as speaker at a time when fears for his safety were specially acute. She had found opportunity to confer with women from every part of the country, whose help was needed for the execution of her plans. That afternoon she intended to get a binding pledge of their cooperation.

The scene in the crowded stuffy room in the basement of the hotel where the Council met is something I shall always remember: the tired faces of most of the women there; the huge map of the United States, hung on one of the

†From: Maud Wood Park, *Front Door Lobby* (Boston: Beacon Press, 1960), pp. 15-18.
Copyright 1960 by Edna Lamprey Stantial. Reprinted by permission of Beacon Press.

walls; and, most vividly of all, Mrs. Catt herself, when, after the routine business of the Council was over, she took up the typed pages in which she had outlined the work of the coming year.

To her preamble, which was a brief restatement of reasons for undertaking a more energetic drive for the amendment, I listened with a good deal of inward protest. I could not forget that the only woman suffrage planks in both the major party platforms called for action by the separate states, not by the Congress. I believed that, hard as the advance, state by state, was bound to be, we had to have a good many more states in which women could vote before the drive for a federal amendment would be successful. Even after Mrs. Catt stated that the Association's Congressional Committee in Washington was to be enlarged and much more spacious headquarters were to be taken there, I was still skeptical.

Then she started to explain that no amount of work in Washington was likely to bring about the submission of the amendment unless new victories were won in the states. At that point I began to listen more carefully, for it was clear that Mrs. Catt had no intention of letting her federal program lessen efforts to secure state action. On the contrary, as I soon learned, her plan was essentially a demand for legislative activity in every part of the country during the coming sessions of the state legislatures.

Pointer in hand, she stepped to the map and traced four divisions of states, to each of which she assigned a particular form of legislative work. First, she called on our organizations in the equal suffrage states and in Illinois to secure from their legislatures resolutions requesting the Congress to submit the woman suffrage amendment. In the case of the income tax amendment, she explained, resolutions from the state legislatures had proved extremely helpful.

Next she pointed out several states—New York among them—in which there was a chance of carrying a state constitutional amendment to enfranchise women. In all those states she urged our workers to prepare at once for a campaign to get their legislatures to submit such an amendment and the voters to support it.

For most of the remaining states she advised trying for presidential suffrage, i.e., the right to vote for presidential electors, which could be given by the legislatures without referring the question to the voters. For a few of the southern one-party states, where success in the primary is equivalent to an election, she told the delegates that they ought to make an attempt to get suffrage in the primaries, a form that could also be granted outright by the state legislatures.

In brief, confronted with the choice between work in state campaigns and work for a federal amendment, Mrs. Catt declared, "We must do both and do them together."

When the fourfold plan had been made clear, she described the procedure necessary to put it into effect. An immediate start upon the work was imperative, she explained, in order to have everything ready at the beginning of the legislative sessions, most of which opened in January. If our campaigns were simultaneous, the opposition, taken by surprise and unprepared for a fight on so many fronts at once, would be forced to concentrate on a few states or else to spread itself too thin to be effective. Then, warning her listeners that the plan would fail if its scope leaked out, she requested from them a definite pledge that they would disclose no details except such as were required in each state for its own project.

Last of all, she presented a compact to be signed by the representatives of suffrage associations in at least thirty-six states. She reminded us that, since thirty-six was the minimum number of states necessary for the ratification of a federal amendment, a failure on the part of a single state would mean ultimate defeat for all.

When the full number of signatures had been affixed to the compact and we filed out of the room, I felt like Moses on the mountain top after the Promised Land had been shown to him and he knew the long years of wandering in the Wilderness were soon to end. For the first time I saw our goal as possible of attainment in the near future. But we had to have swift and concerted action from every part of the country. Could we get it? Could we get it?

Often since then, remembering how hard it was at best to win our vote in the Congress and the subsequent ratification by thirty-six states, I have speculated as to what would have happened if Mrs. Catt's plan had not been presented on that sultry afternoon in 1916. Undoubtedly a woman suffrage amendment would have been adopted at some time, even if Mrs. Catt had never been born; but, if success had not come when it did, the cause might easily have been caught in a period of postwar reaction, and victory postponed for another half-century. That women all over the United States were able to vote in 1920 is due, I believe, to the carrying out of the plan prepared and presented by an incomparable leader.

7-f

Holding the Party in Power Responsible

A major point of difference between NAWSA on the one hand and the Woman's Party on the other was their perception of the American political system. In August 1916 the press chairman of the Woman's Party, in a long letter to *The Outlook* explained why the Woman's Party proposed to oppose all Democrats in the coming presidential election.

Document†

To the Editor of The Outlook: Dear Sir—Will you permit me to say, in answer to your editorials in The Outlook of July 19 on "The Women Voters" and "The Issues as Women See Them," that the vote of the Woman's Party must be reckoned with because a small number of votes constitute the balance of power in each of the twelve suffrage States? The Woman's Party is already completely organized in all of these States, and it has an issue which makes an especial appeal to women.

Of course the entire vote of the four million women qualified to vote for President will not be cast solidly for any one candidate. It is absurd to expect that it will be. It is quite possible, as you estimate, that not more than two million or two million five hundred thousand will actually avail themselves of their opportunity to vote. Fortunately, however, for the hopes of the Woman's Party, neither four million nor even two million votes are necessary to make effective the demand for an amendment to the Constitution enfranchising women.

The suffrage States are close and doubtful territory. During the last five Presidential campaigns an average change of only nine per cent of the vote would have altered the result in every election. The percentages for the five elections are as follows:

	1896.	1900.	1904.	1908.	1912.
California	0.3	0.6	17.4	11.2	0.01
Colorado	34.9	6.7	3.0	0.5	7.8
Idaho	28.4	2.1	20.2	8.4	0.5
Illinois	6.5	4.2	14.2	7.7	0.8
Kansas	4.9	3.3	19.4	4.8	3.2

†From: *The Outlook,* August 23, 1916, pp. 1002-4.

	1896.	1900.	1904.	1908.	1912.
Montana	30.1	9.3	10.2	2.2	3.4
Nevada	28.4	10.9	10.7	1.0	5.9
Oregon	1.0	7.8	23.8	11.0	3.4
Utah	33.3	1.1	14.3	8.5	2.5
Washington	6.7	5.9	25.3	12.9	4.0
Wyoming	0.7	8.5	18.9	7.9	0.9

In 1912 the result in Idaho was determined by 556 votes; in Wyoming, by 376; in California, by 88. In Nevada Senator Newlands was elected to the Senate by 38 votes and Senator Pittman by 88.

It is obvious that the dependence of the Woman's Party need not be in numbers, although, before its campaign has fairly begun, it has tens of thousands of members. Standing apart from and outside of the two great parties, the Woman's Party can hold the balance of power in the States whence come ninety-one electoral votes. The strength of the Woman's Party is not in numbers, but in strategic position.

The Woman's Party is completely organized in each of the twelve suffrage States. It is, in fact, the third party, having possessed itself of the place left vacant by the Progressive Party, but with this advantage—that the Woman's Party vote is concentrated, instead of scattered over the whole United States. The Woman's Party was launched in Chicago, June 5, 6, and 7, at a convention of voting women called by Miss Alice Paul, National Chairman of the Congressional Union for Woman Suffrage. It is made up of voting women pledged to put "suffrage first" in the fall campaign. Upon coming into being the party, under the leadership of Miss Anne Martin, Chairman of the National Committee, took possession of the State organizations perfected during the last three years in the twelve States by the Congressional Union. Since June 7 organization has gone rapidly forward, until now committees have been formed and are at work in almost every county. It is expected that the organization of every county will be complete by August 10, when the first conference to determine election policies convenes in Colorado Springs.

No one who went West in the Suffrage Special can doubt that the Woman's Party has an issue which makes a special appeal to women. Although it is quite true that women, like men, are interested in the European war, our Mexican policy, prohibition, and international questions, yet it is also true that the National Woman Suffrage amendment, usually known as the Susan B. Anthony Amendment, can be made a paramount issue with thousands and thousands of Western women. The reasons why Western women can be so interested are plain. It is only by a Federal amendment that the inter-State and National discrimination against their own political rights can be removed, that Eastern women can be enfranchised, and that Western women can use their political power to bestow the gift of freedom upon others.

Western women want the Susan B. Anthony Amendment because they resent conditions which disfranchise them if they move East to live. They resent laws which take from them their citizenship if they marry aliens. Great hardship is wrought by such laws. In the State of Washington, for instance, an American woman was denied a mother's pension because her husband, who had deserted her and neither seen her nor supported her for years, had become a Canadian. In Illinois an American woman applying for a pension for the blind was refused because she was married to a foreigner. American women lawyers who marry foreigners can no longer practice in our courts. Western women wish to safeguard their citizenship and their political freedom as men's are safeguarded.

Western women desire more influence in shaping National policies. This they cannot possess until all American women count politically. But American women cannot be enfranchised within any reasonable length of time except by an amendment to the Constitution of the United States. Amending State Constitutions is slow, burdensome, and in many States hopeless, because of the difficulties to amendment inherent in the Constitutions of the States.

A State constitutional amendment must usually be passed by a two-thirds vote of the State Legislature, and then submitted to a referendum of the male voters of the State. In New Mexico the proposed amendment must receive a three-fourths vote of the entire Legislature, a three-fourths vote of the entire electorate, and a two-thirds vote of all those voting in each county. In New Hampshire an amendment must be submitted by a constitutional convention, which can be called only once in seven years, and the process of calling it is excessively difficult. The proposed amendment requires for ratification two-thirds of the votes of all electors voting. Indiana requires a majority of the votes of all the qualified electors of the State. It has never been possible to amend the Constitution of Indiana.

Seven States fix a term of years after an amendment has failed of adoption before it can be resubmitted. Four States restrict the number of amendments to be submitted at any election. Eleven States require for the approval of an amendment a majority of all the votes cast at an election, not a majority of the votes cast for or against the particular amendment. In two States the final approval of an amendment is left with the legislators even after the electors have approved of it. These are only a few of the difficulties in the way of amending State Constitutions. Moreover, State work is like trying to progress over shifting sand. An advance once made cannot be held. When a State referendum fails, work must start again from the very beginning.

On the other hand, in work for a Federal amendment every step forward is a permanent gain. A Federal amendment once passed by a two-thirds vote of Congress is passed forever, and needs for ratification only a majority vote of three-fourths of the State Legislatures. Once ratified by a State Legislature, the amendment cannot be brought up again; but, if rejected by the State Legislature, it can be immediately reconsidered.

The Federal method is not only easier, it is also fair. A Federal amendment does not infringe on the rights of a State. Such rights cannot be abridged by using a method prescribed by the Constitution and agreed to by the States. A

Federal amendment simply applies the principle of majority rule, and objections to it lie equally against our whole system of government. A Federal woman suffrage amendment does not complicate the race problem. There are six million more white than colored women living south of Mason and Dixon's line, and two million more white women than Negro men, women, and children combined.

Nor is the Federal method alarmingly novel. The States have never had exclusive control of suffrage. The original Constitution laid down specifications as to who should vote for members of the Senate and who should vote for members of the House of Representatives. The Fifteenth Amendment declared that United States Senators should be elected by the people. Moreover, the Federal Government alters the electorate through its control of naturalization laws. The United States permits foreigners to become citizens. Under the Fifteenth Amendment, it forbids the disfranchisement of these citizens simply because they are foreigners.

Men may regard with complacency the difficulties of the State-by-State road to enfranchisement, toward which women are blandly waved. But women will not accept this impossible way for their sisters when they have a right to proceed in an easier and better way according to established forms of law. Western women thrill to the thought that they have the power to open to their sisters this way to freedom. They realize that their power can be made effective only in pressure upon the National Government. It is a pregnant fact, and very characteristic of the psychology of women, that work for the freedom of women appeals to thousands of women who did not work for their own enfranchisement. And hundreds of women have contributed to the war chest of the Woman's Party who did not contribute to their own State suffrage campaign.

Why should it be called revenge for women who desire the political freedom of others to vote against a party openly unfriendly to the only method by which Nation-wide suffrage for women can be gained? It is no more revenge to vote in the interests of the freedom of *other women* than to vote in the interests of peace and preparedness . . . And why should suffrage as an all-absorbing issue be side-tracked by the women of the West for "Americanism"? There never was a greater opportunity to make "suffrage first" the paramount issue. Both great parties are vociferous in claiming the issues of peace and preparedness. President Wilson, who stands for peace, also toured the country in the interests of military preparedness. The Republican party stands for peace, according to the testimony of Governor Glynn. In his keynote speech at the Democratic Convention Governor Glynn, amid shouts of applause and cries for more, recited the many occasions on which under international provocation leaders of the Republican party had in the past written notes! Certainly the Republican party claims preparedness too. Witness the cartoons of Colonel Roosevelt weeping for his stolen issue and not to be comforted.

In this connection, I must confess that I do not know just precisely what Americanism means. But if it means, as I believe it does, the dedication of all that is best in our beloved country to making this Nation, not only strong and peaceful, but also *just,* then surely there is no reason why Western women should not vote as women in woman's cause of freedom.

ABBY SCOTT BAKER,
Press Chairman Woman's Party.

National Headquarters,
Washington, D.C.

7-g

The Argument for Bipartisanship or Nonpartisanship

Helen Ring Robinson, a state senator in Colorado, explained why the NAWSA thought the Woman's Party was on the wrong track, and why it was necessary to support the friends of suffrage in both parties.

Document†

What About The Woman's Party?

By Helen Ring Robinson
Senator of the State of Colorado

Republican Platform: The Republican party . . . favors the extension of the suffrage to women, but recognizes the right of each state to settle this question for itself.

It is known to all children—and politicians—that a plank makes an excellent see-saw.

It is probable, therefore, that the suffrage planks in the Republican and Democratic platforms were not, in themselves, taken very seriously by the party leaders who put them there. But the danger of not inserting them was taken most seriously. For this reason those two suffrage planks, which declare in effect that the two great national political parties recognize the justice of giving woman the vote—but will not lift a finger to help her—are the greatest tactical gains ever made by the suffrage cause.

Senators Lodge, Penrose, Wadsworth, and representatives of the "interests"—more especially of the breweries, and the big manufacturing interests employing women—stubbornly opposed, as they are, to equal suffrage, could probably have prevented the adoption of the suffrage plank by the Republican convention had they so willed. But their sense of political strategy governed them. They realized that the woman's vote must be considered—almost as if it were the German! James Nugent of New Jersey,

†From: *The Independent*, vol. 87, no. 11. September 1916, pp. 381-82.

Governor Ferguson of Texas, and agents of the whisky interests tried to prevent a suffrage plank being hammered into the Democratic platform. But the great majority of the delegates realized that the time had come when they must give to organized women some of the consideration they allowed to organized labor.

Politically speaking, it is more useful for a woman to be feared than loved!

Two suffrage associations carried on the fight for a suffrage endorsement at Chicago and again at St. Louis: The National Suffrage Association and The Congressional Union. The National Association is laboring to win suffrage either state by state or by a national amendment. It doesn't care which—so long as it gets it. The Congressional Union limits its efforts to securing a national suffrage amendment. Just half the program of the older organization; but it proclaims the half greater than the whole.

The National Association, with its magnificent generalship, got practically what it asked for at the conventions. The Union got what it distinctly did not want. Yet of the two organizations there is little doubt that the Union was the more instrumental in securing the two planks with their high strategic value.

The Congressional Union was extremely practical—for the moment. It did not appeal to the delegates for votes for women; but it shook votes of women in their faces.

There they were. Count them—3,100,000 votes. Or, not to be bigoted over a few figures, let the immitigable declaration of the Congressional Union stand: "Four Million Women Voters!" All in the twelve states: Wyoming, Colorado, Utah, Idaho, California, Washington, Oregon, Arizona, Kansas, Illinois, Nevada and Montana; states representing 91 electoral votes. And remember more than half these voters have been enfranchised since the last presidential election.

Votes enough, surely, to win the respect of any politician if—aye, that's the rub!—if they can be rendered, so to speak, acute. If, in other words, they can affirm solidarity. If they can be mobilized for suffrage purposes.

Can they?

Democratic Platform: We recommend the extension of the franchise to the women of the country by the states upon the same terms as to men.

Enter—the Woman's Party, the alias adopted in the equal suffrage states for the Congressional Union. The Woman's Party has been most efficiently advertised these past months. It held its first national convention in Chicago on the Monday of "convention week" and no politician of consequence was allowed to escape the knowledge that it intended mobilizing its forces as a balance of power in the "free states."

There is something hypnotic to the average politician in the repetition of any impressive series of figures—"Four Million" for example. And that is the reason why the two great political parties committed themselves, platonically, to the suffrage cause.

And now, having triumphed in securing what it did not want, what of the future of the Woman's Party?

A few days after the adjournment of the Democratic National Convention a member of the Woman's Party, with the practical knowledge of political aspects which most of its leaders lack, assured me that the Woman's Party was all drest up—but it had no place to go.

"With the two parties 'favoring' or 'recommending' the extension of the franchise to women on practically identical terms," she said, "what is there for a Woman's Party to do? No party was ever established on the difference between Tweedledum and Tweedledee—tho parties may have been kept going on that difference.

"Certainly to ban the Democratic party for not passing the Federal amendment will be equivalent to blessing the Republican party for declaring in its platform, in effect, that it is opposed to a Federal suffrage amendment." She added, "And that would be to convert the party into a campaign joke."

Such was the situation when Mr. Hughes made his declaration in favor of enfranchising women, as speedily as possible, thru a Federal amendment—a declaration not given, however the official status of a place in the Republican candidate's speech of acceptance.

"That settles it!" came a joyous Republican chorus. "The Woman's Party will declare for Hughes! Four million women voters!"

Wait a bit!

Two years ago when the Congressional Union, for which, as has been shown, the new Woman's Party is an alias, sought the defeat of Democratic senators and congressmen in the equal suffrage states, the leaders answered all protests that these men had long worked for equal suffrage: "It is not a question of individual views. We attack these men because they belong to the party in power that has failed to pass the Federal amendment. The individual is nothing to us; we work with parties!"

So, doubtless impelled by a desire to be consistent, the Woman's Party, at its recent executive conference at Colorado Springs, August 11, contented itself with congratulating Mr. Hughes "on the unequivocal stand which he has taken for human liberty." Then, making no reference to the fact that the Republican party platform expressly states that it has become a states rights party on the suffrage question only, the conference made a declaration of war on the Democratic party because in suffrage, as in other matters, it is a states rights party—more or less!

> Whereas, The present administration under President Wilson and the Democratic party have persistently opposed the passage of a national suffrage amendment;
> Resolved, That the National Woman's party, so long as the opposition of the Democratic party continues, pledges itself to use its best efforts in the twelve states where women vote for President to defeat the Democratic candidate for President, and in the eleven states where women vote for members of Congress to defeat the candidates of the Democratic party for Congress.

The practical question now is, How many votes can the Woman's Party deliver, as a side partner, to the Republican party? Or, to fit the question to the party policy, how many votes can it divert from the Democratic party?

The profession of the prophet is the most dangerous of all human vocations. But I will risk it. The number will be very small. That is not because women voters are unconcerned about the suffrage issue. We women voters want votes for women in all the states. We want this for the sake of other women and we want it for our own sake, also. We know that no American woman is fully enfranchised till all are enfranchised, since a necessary change of residence across state boundaries may lose us our status as voting citizens. We realize, moreover, we women who have so long endured it patiently, that we must continue to be targets for the soul-insulting nonsense of the hirelings of antisuffrage forces until the suffrage question is settled and settled right. Naturally, we are eager to write woman, as well as God, into the constitution of our country.

But such women voters, their intelligence developed and trained thru the exercize of the franchise, realize that the leaders of the Woman's Party confuse the game of politics with mumblety peg.

Take that Colorado Springs declaration. There was the danger, in preparing it, of making one of two blunders.

And of two evils the party leaders chose both.

There was, first, the folly of trying to build up a party, here in America, on purely destructive lines. Such a party might, possibly, be thinkable—for men. But never for women. For women voters are far more practical in their thinking processes than are men.

This fact was aptly exprest the other day, in a published interview by Agnes Riddle, for two terms a member of the lower house of the Colorado General Assembly and now a Republican candidate for the state senate. Mrs. Riddle is a shrewd observer with much political experience and an ardent supporter of Mr. Hughes—but she has no kind words for the Woman's Party propaganda, tho it will, indirectly, help her candidate.

"Spite work won't get you anywhere," she says. "I call it foolish, this business of the women spending their time doing spite work against a party or candidate." And she goes on to describe the "tactics" of the new party as "just plain nagging" and to declare that women, to get anywhere politically, must fight definitely for a party or a policy—not merely destructively.

The second folly was in assuming that the "anti-party" policy, even if successful, could advance the suffrage cause.

A two-thirds vote being necessary, in both houses of Congress, to pass a Federal suffrage amendment, it follows that it is unjust to hold a majority party responsible for the failure of such an amendment—unless it is a two-thirds majority party. No party in the past hundred years has controlled such a majority in Congress. It is a safe estimate that neither party will control such a majority for some years to come.

Even should Mr. Hughes and a Republican Congress be elected—let it be assumed thru the efforts of the Woman's Party—and even should the President succeed in forcing his party in Congress into line for the suffrage amendment (Yes, Senator Weeks and all!) there would still be needed a considerable number of Democratic votes.

Would they be there? Chastened by the anti-party forces but eager to oblige?

Maybe!

But there are those who think it might be too exciting to ask a corpse to oblige with a jig at its own wake—just to please the man who made him a corpse.

However that may be, the suffrage leaders in the "free states" have always opposed the methods now employed by the Congressional Union—alias the Woman's Party. And, tho many Republican women may align themselves, for strategic purposes, with the Woman's Party, and many Independent and Progressive women may vote for Mr. Hughes, for this reason or that, it is becoming increasingly evident that very few Western women will, next November, play—mumblety peg!

8-a

Stirring Up Activity in the Home Districts

The newly elected Sixty Fifth Congress had been called to meet on April 2, 1917. The international situation was tense, but suffragists wanted to be well prepared to take advantage of the special session in the interest of political justice for women. Maud Wood Park therefore wrote a letter to all the NAWSA congressional chairmen in the states outlining what she thought they should be doing.

Document†

March 21, 1917

DEAR CONGRESSIONAL CHAIRMAN:

The 65th Congress has been called together on April 2nd. Although we cannot tell what the extra session may bring forth, we hope that the need of political justice for women will be more apparent than ever before and that openings may arise which we had not foreseen. It is imperative that we should take advantage of every possibility in our favor. For that reason, there is urgent need for activity in the home districts of Members of Congress. Will you therefore please give immediate attention to the following requests.

I. Reports There are several new members with regard to whom we have had no word from their own state. Please send us *immediately* a statement, as full as you are able to make it, about the men whose names are enclosed.

Caution. Although we are most anxious to know how the Members of Congress stand with regard to the Federal Amendment, we beg you to take the utmost care that no Member is allowed to commit himself *against* the Amendment when he can be prevented from doing so. If you think he is inclined to be opposed, let us know your opinion; but in your letters to him and in your interviews, frame your appeals in such a way that they will not offer opportunity for a negative answer.

II. Delegations If time allows and unless you have already done this work, delegations should visit your new Members before they leave for Washington. Delegations should be sent also to the old Members who are reported as

†From: Women's Rights Collection, Schlesinger Library, Radcliffe College, Cambridge, Massachusetts.

"non-committal" or "opposed." Old Members who are in favor should be seen less formally, thanked for their position in the past, and given to understand, in a friendly and cordial way, that we are confident of their continued support.

In this connection, we ought all to remind ourselves constantly that Members expect to be treated as individuals. Do not permit circular letters to be sent them; but in writing or visiting them, be sure to make clear that you differentiate the individual from the group. In the case of friendly men, great harm has been done by writing or speaking as if their previous records were unknown and their support unappreciated.

Care should be taken in forming delegations to choose, if possible, women whose families have political influence in the man's own party and who are representative of the different sections of his district. It is well to have a small group of persons of real importance in the District rather than a large group of less prominent people. Effective use should be made of our recent remarkable gains in Ohio, North Dakota, Indiana and Canada. For example, copies of the maps giving the increase of suffrage territory might be shown and a statement made of our gain in electoral votes.

Please let us know what you are able to do in this matter.

III. Work by Men *Individual Calls.* The best advice that we have been able to get with regard to our work in the coming session bids us lay much more emphasis on *work by men in the home Districts.* We therefore urge you to try to get men of political prominence to call, apparently casually, on your Congressmen before they return to Washington to express to them the hope that they may support the Federal Amendment. The more men you can get to make these calls the better, for they will be enormously effective. They should be quite apart from the delegations.

Committees of Men. While you are seeking men to make these personal calls, it would be well also to start in each Congressional District a committee or group of men prominent in politics or in other ways who will agree to help as the need may arise by sending letters and telegrams to the Congressmen. When such a committee or group has been formed, a list of its members with addresses should be sent to our office with the name of the District Congressional Chairman through whom they can be reached. Mrs. Catt in her letter of March 12th wrote you in this connection. We are merely reminding you and urging you to make every effort to secure as many influential men as possible for these committees.

IV. Completion of State Congressional Committees Mrs. Catt also urged you to complete your list of District Congressional Chairmen, if such list is not already filled. The Chairman of each District should make herself responsible for the accumulation of all information with regard to her Congressman which could possibly be of use to the workers in Washington. She should know about his political, social and personal standing, what influences effected his election, what pressure he would most quickly feel, his previous record in Congress and any earlier political record he may have. If he is a former member of the State Legislature, she should know what kind of bills he sponsored in the legislature and whether he is progressive or reactionary with regard to social and humanitarian measures. In short, she should know all about him, and most important of all, she should pass that information on to us in Washington in order that we may make the best possible use of it.

Special. In addition to your chairman for each Congressional District, you should appoint two members "at large" each of whom should hold herself responsible for one of your Senators in the same manner in which the Congressional District Chairman is responsible for the Representative from her District. Will you kindly send us the names of those two members-at-large as soon as possible?

V. State Organization Work When your State is planning its organization work, can you not arrange with the State Organization Committee to put its full force into the Districts whose Representatives in Congress are on your "doubtful" list? It is possible that the reason why that Representative is "doubtful" is that the suffrage organization in his District is weak. If you could send an organizer into that District to stir up new suffrage sentiment or to make articulate and effective the feeling that is already there, the man might be swung into our ranks for the coming session. If you can accomplish this with even one of your "doubtful" men, you will have done much toward the end which we are all hoping to attain in this coming Congress. We look to the State Congressional Chairmen and their lieutenants in the Congressional District to make this hope an accomplished fact.

Summary We shall then expect from you:

I. An immediate report on the new members whose names are enclosed.

II. An early report of any delegations that you are able to arrange.

III. A list of members of your men's committees with their addresses.

IV. The names of the two members-at-large on your State Congressional Committee and the names of any District Chairmen who may have been appointed since your last report to us.

Your National Committee hopes to hear from you more frequently during the coming year. We are convinced that our fighting strength must lie chiefly in a connection with our state organizations represented by the State Congressional Chairmen. We urge you, therefore, to share with us freely all the wisdom which you may have. Your suggestions and criticism at any time, as well as your active co-operation, will be heartily appreciated.

Very cordially yours,
MAUD WOOD PARK, Chairman
RUTH WHITE, Secretary
National Congressional Committee

8-b

"The Fearless Spirit of Youth..."

One of the differences between NAWSA and the Woman's Party lay in the way the members of each saw themselves. NAWSA women believed in being solid, knowledgeable, highly organized and diplomatic. Woman's Party members were more inclined to see themselves as warriors. Lavinia L. Dock of Pennsylvania, 60 years old, was an often-arrested member of the Woman's Party. She was a trained nurse, and had worked at the Henry Street Settlement in New York. In all, she served forty-three days in prison for her suffrage activities. Her article, reprinted here from the Woman's Party newspaper, gives a good sense of how many Woman's Party members saw themselves.

Document†

The Young Are At The Gates

If any one says to me: "Why the picketing for Suffrage?" I should say in reply, "Why the fearless spirit of youth? Why does it exist and make itself manifest?"

Is it not really that our whole social world would be likely to harden and toughen into a dreary mass of conventional negations and forbiddances—into hopeless layers of conformity and caste, did not the irrepressible energy and animation of youth, when joined to the clear-eyed sham-hating intelligence of the young, break up the dull masses and set a new pace for laggards to follow?

What is the potent spirit of youth? Is it not the spirit of revolt, of rebellion against senseless and useless and deadening things? Most of all, against injustice, which is of all stupid things the stupidest?

Such thoughts come to one in looking over the field of the Suffrage campaign and watching the pickets at the White House and at the Capitol, where sit the men who complacently enjoy the rights they deny to the women at their gates. Surely, nothing but the creeping paralysis of mental old age can account for the phenomenon of American men, law-makers, officials, administrators, and guardians of the peace, who can see nothing in the

†From: *The Suffragist*, June 30, 1917.

intrepid young pickets with their banners, asking for bare justice but common obstructors of traffic, naggers—nuisances that are to be abolished by passing stupid laws forbidding and repressing to add to the old junk-heap of laws which forbid and repress? Can it be possible that any brain cells not totally crystallized could imagine that giving a stone instead of bread would answer conclusively the demand of the women who, because they are young, fearless, eager, and rebellious, are fighting and winning a cause for all women—even for those who are timid, conventional, and inert?

A fatal error—a losing fight. The old stiff minds must give way. The old selfish minds must go. Obstructive reactionaries must move on. The young are at the gates!

LAVINIA DOCK.
The Suffragist, June 30, 1917.

8-C

Making Use of Every Opportunity

Even the hard work of lobbying was not without its lighter moments. In later years Maud Wood Park recalled an episode in which suffrage workers tried to make the best use they could of a funeral.

Document†

One of the most entertaining episodes in our work I didn't venture to include in *FRONT DOOR LOBBY*. It had to do with the Congressional delegation which went to Kentucky for the funeral of Senator Ollie James. After he had been in hospital for some time, Senator Ransdell, seeing me in the Senate waiting room one day, sat down beside me and began to talk with a markedly apologetic air. "I'm going to suggest something that may shock you," he said, "but we have to face facts and we all know Senator James cannot live much longer. It has therefore occurred to me that we ought to think of some way to persuade Governor Stanley, who will appoint a temporary successor, to choose a man who will vote for the Amendment. So if we can arrange to have the funeral delegation made up of senators and representatives who are in favor they could talk with the Governor about the President's wish to have the Amendment passed right away. Of course the Governor has always been opposed to woman suffrage, but I understand he wants to come to the Senate himself in the regular election and he'll realize that the President's support would be a great help."

I didn't need to be told that Governor Stanley was opposed, for I remembered that he and Ollie James and Campbell Cantrill were said to be the three men who had been responsible for the defeat in the Kentucky Legislature of the resolution for a State woman suffrage amendment; also that when Mr. Cantrill was converted and voted in Washington for the Federal Amendment, Ollie James was reported as remarking, "Jesus Christ himself must have appeared to Campbell Cantrill to make him come out for woman suffrage."

Since one of the trio had changed to our side I thought it not impossible to get a second. So Senator Ransdell and I made out a list of desirable members for the delegation and then did our best to get them to request an appointment when the time came. Thanks to Senator Ransdell's tactful efficiency, the plan was carried out.

†From: "Congressional Work for the Nineteenth Amendment: Supplementary Notes," Women's Rights Collection, Schlesinger Library, Radcliffe College, Cambridge, Massachusetts.

Before the delegates started I asked several of our friends to telegraph me the result of their talks with the Governor; but the telegrams all reported non-committal replies. I was therefore greatly disappointed until Mr. Cantrill, who had not telegraphed, returned and telephoned a request for me to go to his office immediately. Then he explained, "I didn't try to talk with the Governor at Frankfort but I rode back to Louisville with him and we cussed each other out all the way. So if you don't get a vote from the interim Senator it won't be for lack of cuss words. But I think you will."

And we did: for the appointee, a young man named Martin, voted for the Amendment during his term and Stanley himself supported us after his election to the Senate. Once when I was in Kentucky years later he made a speech at a dinner given for me, a speech filled with glowing words about the success of woman suffrage and virtually implying that he had always been a friend of the cause.

My own Congressional work I summarized in my letter to Inez Irwin, March 1933, as follows:

"In general my work was to keep our friends in the Congress active for the Amendment, to direct pressure of every sort upon doubtful or opposed men, to make an accurate poll (Curtis once paid me the compliment of asking me to come in every morning to go over the poll on a League of Women Voters' measure which he was pushing because, as he said, he had learned in the suffrage struggle that my information could be depended on), to study the floor situation and to be ready to take advantage of favorable opportunities and to avert threatening action, to keep in touch with friendly politicians in all parts of the country and with leaders of the political parties in Washington, to bring in delegations of our women from states from which we needed help, to stimulate the sending of letters and telegrams at the *right* moment and to hold them back when they might seem too concerted or be likely to do harm in other ways."

I failed to add, though I should have done so, that Helen Gardener's help was my greatest asset.

MAUD WOOD PARK
February 1943.

9-a

The Education of Woodrow Wilson

By the fall of 1918 suffragists had no more dedicated ally than the president of the United States. Woodrow Wilson had not always supported suffrage, nor had his views of women accorded with those of women's rights supporters. These excerpts trace his changing thought, and illustrate something about the wider changes occurring in American social thought between 1885 and 1920.

"The question of higher education of women is certain to be settled in the affirmative, in this country at least, whether my sympathy be enlisted or not . . ."

W.W. to Ellen Axson, Nov. 30, 1885,
Axson-Wilson Letters.

"Lecturing to young women of the present generation on the history and principles of politics is about as appropriate and profitable as would be lecturing to stonemasons on the evolution of fashion in dress. There is a painful *absenteeism* of mind on the part of the audience. Passing through a vacuum, your speech generates no heat. Perhaps it is some of it due to undergraduateism, not all to femininity.

Confidential Journal, Oct. 20, 1887,
The Papers of Woodrow Wilson, edited by Arthur S. Link et al,
sponsored by the Woodrow Wilson Foundation and
Princeton University: selections from vol. 5
(© 1968 by Princeton University Press), p. 619.

"My teaching here this year lies altogether in the field of political economy, and in my own special field of public law: and I already feel that teaching such topics to women threatens to relax not a little my mental muscle—to exalt the function of commonplace rudiments in my treatment."

November 7, 1887, W.W. to James Burrill Angell,
Link, *Papers,* vol. 5, p. 626.

"It distresses me very deeply that the University of Virginia should think, even through a minority of its faculty, of admitting women to its courses. I have had just enough experience of co-education to know that, even under the most favorable circumstances, it is most demoralizing. It seems to me that in the South it would be fatal to the standards of delicacy as between men & women which we most value. . . . I can only pray that the University may be led away from such gratuitous folly!"

W.W. to Charles W. Kent, May 29, 1894, Link, *Papers,*
vol. 8 (© 1970 by Princeton University Press), pp. 583-584.

To Governor Foss of Massachusetts at the opening of the campaign in 1912 advising against injecting the woman suffrage question:

"It is not a national question, but a state question. So far as it is a state question, I am heartily in favour of its thorough discussion & shall never be jealous of its submission to the popular vote. My own judgment in the matter is in an uncertain balance, I mean my judgment as a voting citizen."

Ray S. Baker, *Woodrow Wilson: Life and Letters*
(New York: Doubleday, Doran and Co., 1913), vol. III, p. 385.

In office, he met a group of suffragists:

Document†

... As we have already seen, he had been in his earlier years opposed to votes for women, but had been partially converted through the ardent representations of his daughters. In November, 1913, the powerfully organized suffragists began a serious agitation in Washington. A delegation of seventy-three, by "a good-humoured show of force," invaded the Executive Office on November 17th, and Wilson promised to give the subject earnest attention. He did not, however, mention the matter in his annual address in December. The suffragists were greatly displeased and a few days later sent a delegation of about one hundred women to see him, with Dr. Anna Howard Shaw as spokesman. He was charged, on this occasion, with "dodging the issue": but Dr. Shaw said of the interview:

"I inquired if I might ask him a question. He said I might. I said: 'Mr. President, since you cannot present our case to Congress, and since we have no committee in the House, who is to speak for us there?' He returned laughingly that he had found us well able to speak for ourselves, whereupon I said: 'But not authoritatively. Have we anyone, Mr. President, to present our case with authority to Congress?' He hesitated a moment, the muscles of his face twitched; I was dreadfully frightened myself, and I do believe he was as much frightened; but he didn't evade the question; he answered squarely, 'No.' "

After leaving the White House, Dr. Shaw said optimistically of the visit:

"It was all that we could ask for. He is in favour of a committee of the House; that was our chief purpose in coming to see him."

On the other hand, he was having to meet the opposition of violent anti-suffragists who were small in number, but active, and we find a number of letters to them.

In February of the next year the campaign continued still more vigorously. A large delegation of working women, headed by Mrs. Glendower Evans of Boston, came, with banners inscribed with phrases from Wilson's speeches. According to the New York *Times*, Mr. Wilson greeted them "pleasantly and smilingly." He tried to impress them with the limitations upon his time and

†Baker, *Woodrow Wilson*, vol. IV, pp. 225-226.

strength, and the importance of the great questions in which he was then absorbed. He also declared that he was "subject to certain limitations which restrict me to speaking only for what my party has declared"—a statement criticized for being "an excuse, not a reason," since he was supporting various other proposals for which his party had not declared.

Headline, *New York Times:*

NEW JERSEY BEATS SUFFRAGE BY 46,278
PRESIDENT WILSON VOTES "Yes"

In the body of the story, the *Times* reported:

President Wilson voted in the Seventh Precinct of Princeton Borough. The vote cast in that district stood 64 for the Amendment and 160 against, a majority of almost 100 . . .

Mrs. Galt, the President's fiancee, while Mr. Wilson was on his way to Princeton to vote "Yes" let it be known in Washington that she is opposed to women voting . . .

New York Times, October 20, 1915.

"The plank [in the Democratic platform supporting suffrage state by state] received my hearty approval . . . and I shall support its principle with sincere pleasure . . . "

July 22, 1916, Telegram to the National Board of NAWSA.
Catt and Shuler, *Woman Suffrage and Politics*
(New York: Charles Scribner's Sons, 1926), p. 258.

" . . . if I should change my personal attitude now, I should seem to the country like nothing less than an angler for votes, because . . . my attitude in this matter has again and again been very frankly avowed . . .

I have all along believed and still believe, that the thing can best and most solidly be done by the action of the individual states, and that the time it will take to get it that way will not be longer than the time it would take to get it the other way."

W.W. to Mrs. E.P. Davis, August 5, 1916,
Baker, *Woodrow Wilson,* vol. VI, p. 277 fn.

[Regretting the partisan use of the suffrage issue] "at a time so critical as this when the question is about to be determined whether we shall keep the nation upon its present terms of peace and good will with the world or turn to radical changes of policy which may alter the whole aspect of the nation's life."

W.W. to Women's Democratic Club of Portland, Oregon,
September 27, 1916, Baker, *Woodrow Wilson,*
vol. VI, p. 274 fn.

When the Just Government League of Maryland called upon the president to send a message to the Governor and General Assembly endorsing a bill to confer suffrage upon the women of Maryland, Wilson wrote to his secretary Joseph Tumulty:

"The real answer to this letter I think it would perhaps be better for you to write than me. It is that I believe that such action as they suggest would do the cause more harm than good. As a one-time member of the Jersey legislature I think you can yourself imagine how you would feel about a letter from the President of the United States urging action by the State legislature in the way of domestic policy of this sort. I am sure you know how to intimate this difficulty to the ladies."

April 24, 1917, Baker,
Woodrow Wilson, vol. VII, pp. 34-35.

Congratulating Mrs. Catt and NAWSA upon the adoption of presidential suffrage in North Dakota:

"As you know, I have a very real interest in the extension of suffrage to the women, and I feel every step in this direction should be applauded."

W.W. to C.C.C., Jan. 25, 1917,
Carrie Chapman Catt Papers,
Library of Congress, Washington, D.C.

"My attention has been called to the question as to whether it was desirable to appoint a Committee on Woman Suffrage in the House of Representatives. . . . On the chance that I may be of slight service in this matter which seems to me of very considerable consequence, I am writing this line to say that I would heartily approve. I think it would be a very wise act of public policy, and also an act of fairness to the best women who are engaged in the cause of woman suffrage."

W.W. to Representative E.W. Pou,
Chairman of the House Rules Committee,
May 14, 1917, Baker, Woodrow Wilson, vol. VII, pp. 68-69

"May I without taking too great a liberty suggest to you that it would be a very wise thing, both politically and from other points of view, if you and the others in Congress who feel like you would consent to the constitution of a special committee of the House on woman suffrage? I perhaps am more in the storm center of this question than you are, and I think I can give this as my mature counsel; and I am sure that you will understand why I do it and forgive me if I have taken too great a liberty."

W.W. to Representative Thomas Heflin of Alabama,
June 13, 1917, Baker, Woodrow Wilson, vol. VII, p. 109.

"May I not express to you my very deep interest in the campaign in New York for the adoption of woman suffrage . . . I am very anxious to see the great state of New York set an example in this matter."

W.W. to Carrie Chapman Catt, October 13, 1917,
Baker, Woodrow Wilson, vol. VII, p. 306.

"I am very glad to add my voice to those which are urging the people of the great State of New York to set a great example by voting for woman suffrage . . . "

W.W. to a delegation from the New York Woman Suffrage Party,
October 25, 1917, Baker, Woodrow Wilson, vol. VII, p. 324.

Theodore Roosevelt in a letter written today to William R. Willcox, chairman of the Republican National Committee, urges that everything be done in the Republican organization to get the Republican congressmen to vote in favor of the constitutional amendment giving women suffrage. He also advocates the addition to the National Committee of a woman member from every suffrage state. The letter follows:

"I earnestly hope that the Republican Party as such will do everything possible to get all its representatives in Congress to vote in favor of the constitutional amendment giving women suffrage. This is no longer an academic question. The addition of New York to the suffrage column, I think, entitles us to say that as a matter of both justice and of common sense the nation should no longer delay to give women suffrage. Will you also let me urge as strongly as possible that there be an immediate addition to the Republican National Committee of one woman member from every suffrage state? I do hope this action can be taken."

New York Times, January 4, 1918, p. 11.

"The committee found that the President had not felt at liberty to volunteer his advice to members of Congress in this important matter, but when we sought his advice he very frankly and earnestly advised us to vote for the amendment as an act of right and justice to the women of the country and of the world."

Statement written by the president and handed to newspapermen after an interview with a number of Democratic members of the House, January 9, 1918, Baker, *Woodrow Wilson,* vol. VII, p. 458.

Jowett Shouse, Assistant Secretary of the Treasury, urged the president to call prominent men from various southern delegations to the White House and appeal to them to lay aside their personal prejudices and, for the sake of the party, vote for the woman suffrage amendment.

"It is extremely hard to reply to generous letters like yours ... without seeming to do violence to my real personal sentiments, but the most I have felt at liberty to do (for reasons I am sure you know) has been to give my advice to members of Congress when they have asked for it. Not as many have asked as I could wish. When they do ask, you know what the advice is.

Personally, I am not afraid of the strategy of the Republican management. It can be counted upon to be stupid, and it is always stupid to be insincere, as in this instance I am sure it is."

W.W. to Shouse, January 9, 1918, Baker, *Woodrow Wilson,* vol. VII, p. 460.

"It was supposed, as you say in your letter ... that there were 'half a dozen possibilities' in the Senate from whom we might draw sufficient support to put the federal amendment through, but as a matter of fact I have done my best to draw from that half-dozen and have utterly failed. We have left nothing undone that I can think of which could have been wisely or sufficiently done . . . "

W.W. to Mrs. George Bass, May 22, 1918,
Baker, *Woodrow Wilson*, vol. VIII, p. 157.

Between June 4, 1918 and September 26, Wilson wrote to eight southern senators and September 26 and 27 telegraphed appeals to six. The following letter to Senator Christie Benet of South Carolina is one of the strongest:

"I know that you will forgive and justify me as leader of our party in making another direct and very earnest appeal to you to vote for the suffrage amendment.

"I need not assure you that I would not venture to make this direct appeal to you, were I not convinced that affirmative action on the amendment is of capital importance not only to the party, but to the country, and to the maintenance of the war spirit and the support of the administration which is indispensable to the winning of the war.

"It would take me a long time, my dear Senator Benet, to tell you in detail upon what evidence I have reached this conviction. I am sure that you will not require of me that I should detail the evidence. I can say that my conviction is founded upon impressions received from many directions upon which I am sure I can rely, for I have tested them in many ways."

W.W. to Senator Christie Benet, September 18, 1918,
Baker, *Woodrow Wilson*, vol. VIII, p. 412.

The Senate, nevertheless, on October 1 failed by two votes to supply the required two-thirds. On October 3 a delegation of suffrage leaders called to thank him for his effort:

"I do not deserve your gratitude . . . when my conversion to this idea came, it came with an overwhelming command that made it necessary that I should omit nothing and use the position I occupied to enforce it, if I could possibly do so . . . history will deal very candidly with the circumstances in which the head of a Government asked the kind of support that I asked the other day, and did not get it . . . I have to restrain myself sometimes from intellectual contempt. That is a sin, I am afraid, and being a good Presbyterian, I am trying to refrain from it. . . . "

The address was taken down by a stenographer, and the women asked permission to have it published. This, however, the president thought inadvisable . . .

Baker, *Woodrow Wilson*, vol. VIII, p. 446.

9-b

"Nothing Has Been Left Undone..."

The night before the suffragists' last effort with the Sixty-Fifth Congress Carrie Chapman Catt wrote to Maud Wood Park indicating that she was quite prepared for the vote to go either way ... the letter reprinted below gives a good feel for the relationship between the two NAWSA leaders in the tension of the last days.

Document†

Feb. 9, 1919.

My dear Maud:

Apparently our chances have not been changed except by the additional earnestness of our friends and bitterness of our foes. Mollie thinks the chances equal. Well, if fate perches victory on our bedraggled and outworn banner, we shall all be glad and perhaps we shall even feel jubilant. We shall shed no tears at any rate. But if our familiar experience is repeated, I want you to know that I am quite resigned and I think to the point that I shall not suffer. Editorials if and if are written and ready for the Citizen. Mrs. Shuler is bringing the telegrams to send out if we go through and bulletins if we do and if we don't are ready too. In any event the delay cannot be long. Those who will eventually triumph can afford to be patient and forgiving.

I wish I might put you in a very tender embrace and steady your nerve and courage for these next days. If it is a go, you will steady yourself with joy, but if it isn't it will be a temporary shock and disturber of poise, which if I could I would ease for you.

If through we go, dance a jig and go to bed for a week of sweet sleep. If through we don't go, swear a few swears and go to bed and sleep a week just the same. If through we go, it was you who did it; if through we don't go, no other human being could have put it through. Nothing has been left undone, except the Lord's creation of certain creatures who pass for statesmen. *He might* have done a better job!

So many of our officers are curious to see those queer Senators, inspired by much the same curiosity as the public by the ads of the Wild Man, that someone must stay home with finger on the trigger while they look through the bars of the senatorial cage. At the same time I am mending my physical incapacities so as to be in better trim for the next battle and I therefore will not be down for the Victory Dinner.

†From: Carrie Chapman Catt to Maud Wood Park, Feb. 9, 1919, Women's Rights Collection, Schlesinger Library, Radcliffe College, Cambridge, Massachusetts.

With the most loving and complete confidence one human being can feel for another, I am

Yours for victory
Yours for defeat
Yours anyway
(signed) CARRIE CHAPMAN CATT

9-C

"The Passage of the Amendment Depends Upon Your Work..."

Maud Wood Park's letter of May 14, 1919 to the congressional chairmen in each state conveys the sense of urgency suffragists felt as they approached the Senate vote to take place on June 4.

Document†

CONGRESSIONAL COMMITTEE
HEADQUARTERS
1626 RHODE ISLAND AVENUE
WASHINGTON, D.C.
Secretary Press, MISS MARJORIE SHULER

May 14, 1919.

Dear Congressional Chairman:

This is a RUSH request to fill an imperative NEED. The newspaper reports that the federal amendment is sure of passage have turned tremendous anti-pressure upon the members of both houses. This is the crisis. The passage of the amendment depends upon YOUR work in holding the men already pledged and turning the doubtful ones to our side. Will you do the following things?

DOUBTFUL MEMBERS. Here is your most important task. Please organize to get all possible pressure and many letters and telegrams to these men, beginning the first day of the session, May 19th and continuing until the vote is taken.

NEW MEMBERS, FRIENDS. Next in importance is sending all possible letters and telegrams to these men telling them that their aid is counted upon.

OLD MEMBERS, FRIENDS. If you have not already made clear to these men that you are counting on their votes and therefore have asked their constituents not to bother them with letters [make sure a letter to that] effect is sent before the end of next week.

†From: Women's Rights Collection, Schlesinger Library, Radcliffe College, Cambridge, Massachusetts.

NEW MEMBERS, OPPONENTS. As much pressure and as many letters and telegrams as possible should be brought to bear upon these men, since there is always more hope of those not recorded as having previously voted against us.

OLD MEMBERS, OPPONENTS. Do as much work on these men as your patience and energy permit.

We are trying to secure a vote within the first ten days of the session. Whether we can get our friends among the absentees in Europe and elsewhere back within this time is still a question.

The situation requires prompt attention. YOUR work may assure the victory. Please take none but those committed in writing for granted as pledged to vote for us. Please take none but those most bitterly opposed for granted as being hopelessly against us. Success to you.

Cordially yours,
MAUD WOOD PARK
Congressional Chairman.

9-d

Four Factors Making for Success

In 1933 Maud Wood Park and Inez Haynes Irwin had some correspondence about the movement in which each had played an important part, though in rival organizations. Park explained her view of why the success came when it did.

Document†

Congressional Work For Nineteenth Amendment.

Introductory Note

(Excerpt from letter of Maud Wood Park to Inez Haynes Irwin, March, 1933).

"In my judgment there were four factors responsible for our success at the time it came:

. "1st and *foremost:* Mrs. Catt's plan for a nationwide campaign announced in a closed conference, every person present being required to give a pledge of absolute secrecy, at the Atlantic City Convention in September 1916, (the convention at which President Wilson gave the first tacit pledge to support the Federal Amendment).

"2nd, The victory in New York State, for which Mary Garrett Hay deserves much of the credit on account of her organization of the Woman Suffrage Party in the City and her clever tactics with Tammany, with the incredible result that the majority in the City was large enough to offset the deficit upstate.

"3rd, The extraordinary ability of Helen Gardener, who was vice-chairman of the National American Woman Suffrage Association's Congressional Committee during the time that I was Chairman. Whatever I was able to do that was of service I owe primarily to her advice and help. She had the most uncanny understanding of the motives, the weaknesses and foibles of the men with whom we were working, combined with great tact and the power to make friends in high places for the cause. We used to call her 'the diplomatic

---

†From: "Excerpt from letter of Maud Wood Park to Inez Haynes Irwin, March 1933," Women's Rights Collection, Schlesinger Library, Radcliffe College, Cambridge, Massachusetts.

corps' of our committee. She was our constant messenger to the White House, for both the President and Tumulty had great liking and admiration for her, as had Champ Clark, Secretary Daniels and many, many others.

"4th, The supposedly impossible defeat of Senator Weeks in Massachusetts."

MAUD WOOD PARK
March 1943.

9-e

Patterns of Congressional Votes

The tables below represent a computer analysis of roll-call data supplied by the Inter-University Corsortium for Political Research, Historical Archive, University of Michigan. Some of the changes revealed by the various cross-tabulations are those one would expect; others—such as the steady increase in yea votes from nonsuffrage states—suggest the changing climate of opinion.

Table I
Impact of State Suffrage on Vote of State Delegations in Congress

Date of vote	% of members from suffrage states voting yea	% of members from nonsuffrage states voting yea	Total vote
Senate			
March 9, 1914	90.0	34.7	35 yea 34 nay
Oct. 1, 1918	95.0	34.0	53 yea 31 nay
Feb. 1, 1919	87.4	31.4	54 yea 30 nay
June 4, 1919	91.4	52.2	56 yea 25 nay
House			
Jan. 12, 1915	95.1	36.6	174 yea 204 nay
Jan. 10, 1918	90.6	49.6	274 yea 136 nay
May 21, 1919	92.2	53.3	304 yea 89 nay

Note: The roll call votes charted here took place in the Sixty-Third, Sixty-Fifth and Sixty-Sixth Congress; the figures are based on yea and nay votes. Pairs were used in both houses. In June 1919, for example, every member of the Senate who did not vote was paired.

The actual numbers of members representing suffrage states changed every time a new state adopted suffrage, but the percentage of members from such states never fell below 87.4%—bearing out the NAWSA contention that the best way to win votes for the federal amendment was to convert more and more state legislatures and state electorates. However, the general change in the climate of opinion is reflected in the sharp increase in the percentage of members from nonsuffrage states who voted for the amendment, particularly in 1919.

Table II
Regional Votes on Suffrage:
Percentage of Regional Delegations Voting Yea

Date of vote	N.E.	Mid-At	ENC	WNC	South	Border	Mt.	Pacific
				Senate				
March 19, 1914	22.2	25	83.3	80	14.3	25	75	100
Oct. 1, 1918	36.4	16.7	87.5	84.6	31.6	77.8	92.3	100
Feb. 10, 1919	36.4	28.6	90	92.3	35	80	92.9	75
June 4, 1919	50	40	100	84.6	29.4	71.4	93.3	100
				House				
Jan. 12, 1915	42.9	51.4	56.6	74	2.3	40.5	91.7	100
Jan. 10, 1918	59.4	74.4	81.5	96.4	18.9	68.4	100	100
May 21, 1919	76.9	84.2	94	98.2	30.1	82.1	100	100

N.E. (New England): Connecticut, Maine, Massachusetts, New Hampshire, Rhode Island, Vermont
Mid-At (Mid-Atlantic): Delaware, New Jersey, New York, Pennsylvania
ENC (East North Central): Illinois, Indiana, Michigan, Ohio, Wisconsin
WNC (West North Central): Iowa, Kansas, Minnesota, Missouri, Nebraska, North Dakota, South Dakota
South: Virginia, Alabama, Arkansas, Florida, Georgia, Louisiana, Mississippi, North Carolina, South Carolina, Texas
Border: Kentucky, Maryland, Oklahoma, Tennessee, West Virginia
Mt. (Mountain): Arizona, Colorado, Idaho, Montana, Nevada, New Mexico, Utah, Wyoming
Pacific: California, Oregon, Washington

Note: The regional breakdown reveals the dramatic change which was taking place in the South. The apparent decline in southern votes for suffrage between February and June 1919 is accounted for by 1) the replacement of one South Carolina senator who was a suffragist by one who was not, 2) an increase in the number of pairs in the June vote. The point to watch is that whereas in January 1918 suffrage votes came from only three southern states, by June 1919 there was at least one such vote from ten southern states. The other dramatic change has been noted on Table III: the newly elected Senators and Representatives were heavily in favor of suffrage. Of 110 new representatives who had taken their seats by the time of the vote in May 1919, only six voted no. Of thirteen new Senators, only two voted no. NAWSA's careful work in the congressional districts was beginning to pay off.

Table III
How the Parties Divided on Suffrage Amendment

Date of vote	Democrats	Republicans	Minor Parties
	Senate		
March 19, 1914 63rd Cong., 2d. sess. (51 Democrats, 43 Republicans, 1 Progressive)	14 yea 22 nay	21 yea 12 nay	
Oct. 1, 1918 65th Cong., 2d. sess., (52 Democrats, 43 Republicans, 1 Progressive)	26 yea 21 nay	27 yea 10 nay	
Feb. 10, 1919 65th Cong., 3d sess. (51 Democrats, 44 Republicans, 1 Progressive)	24 yea 18 nay	30 yea 12 nay	
June 4, 1919[4] 66th Cong., 1st. sess. (47 Democrats, 48 Republicans, 1 Progressive)	20 yea 17 nay	36 yea 8 nay	
	House		
Jan. 12, 1915 63rd. Cong., 3d sess. (283 Democrats, 121 Republicans, 21 minor)	86 yea 170 nay	77 yea 34 nay	11 yea
Jan. 10, 1918 65th Cong., 2d sess., (209 Democrats, 212 Republicans, 7 minor)	102 yea 101 nay[1]	163 yea 34 nay	7 yea 1 nay
May 21, 1919[3] 66th Cong., 1st sess. (191 Democrats, 237 Republicans, 4 minor)	100 yea 70 nay[2]	199 yea 19 nay	5 yea

1. 90 of these from the South
2. 58 of these from the South
3. of 110 new members who had taken their seats only 6 voted no
4. of thirteen new members, only two voted no.

10

The Suffragists: A Collective Sketch

Document†

What were the characteristics of the leading suffragists?

The editors of *Notable American Women* deal with eighty-nine women whose primary claim to being notable was their suffrage activity. Many other women included in this biographical dictionary were suffragists, but their primary contribution lay elsewhere. The eighty-nine provide the basis for this collective sketch. It should be added that *Notable American Women* did not include women who were alive in 1950.

These women were born between 1792 and 1886, with the heaviest concentration of births (thirty-seven) between 1841 and 1870. The decade in which the largest number were born (seventeen) was 1821-1830.

By nineteenth-century standards these suffragists were exceedingly well-educated. At a time when only a tiny percentage of all American women had been to some institution of higher learning, over fifty percent of the suffragists had. A number of those who did not have advanced schooling studied independently or were tutored by husbands or fathers, not infrequently in the law.

Three out of four of the suffragists were married at least once. The average age of marriage was twenty-four years and the modal age was twenty-two, which was very close to the national pattern. The average age of marriage is skewed upward slightly by one doughty suffragist who married for the first time at the age of eighty-seven.

Sixteen percent of the marriages ended in divorce, a higher rate than that of the population at large in 1900.

Of the sixty-seven suffragists who married, fifty-three had children. There were a number of what might be called typical nineteenth-century families of six to eight children but the average number of children was three, well below the national norm for the time.

Seventy-two of the suffragists were affiliated with a national suffrage organization: twenty-five were members of the National Woman's Suffrage

†Data drawn from: Edward and Janet James, eds., *Notable American Women* (Cambridge: The Belknap Press of Harvard University Press, 1971), 3 vols.

Association, fifteen of the American Woman's Suffrage Association, twenty-six of the National American (after the merger) and seven were members of the Woman's Party.

A little over half the women came from families in which the men were active in politics; a third of all the married women had husbands who were politically involved. Five had activist mothers, and five had mothers or daughters who were also included in *Notable American Women*.

The characteristics which seem to distinguish these suffragists from other middle class American women, then, are primarily education and small families. Much more detailed analysis would have to be made before we could say anything about common patterns of motivation or experience, but these facts throw some light on the rapid growth in numbers which occurred in the early twentieth century as general educational levels rose and average numbers of children declined in the middle class.

11

The Electoral Thermometer

Document†

*Woman Suffrage Won by State Constitutional Amendments
and Legislative Acts Before the Proclamation of
the 19th Amendment*

		Electoral Vote
1890	WYOMING was admitted to statehood with woman suffrage, having had it as a territory since 1869.	3
1893	COLORADO adopted a constitutional amendment after defeat in 1877.	6
1896	IDAHO adopted a constitutional amendment on its first submission.	4
1896	UTAH after having woman suffrage as a territory since 1870 was deprived of it by the Congress in 1887, but by referendum put it back in the constitution when admitted to statehood.	4
1910	WASHINGTON adopted a constitutional amendment after defeats in 1889 and 1898. It had twice had woman suffrage by enactment of the territorial legislature and lost it by court decisions.	7
1911	CALIFORNIA adopted a constitutional amendment after defeat in 1896.	13
1912	OREGON adopted a constitutional amendment after defeats in 1884, 1900, 1906, 1908, 1910.	5
1912	KANSAS adopted a constitutional amendment after defeats in 1867 and 1893.	10
1912	ARIZONA adopted a constitutional amendment submitted as a result of referendum petitions.	3
1913	ILLINOIS was the first state to get presidential suffrage by legislative enactment.	29

†From: The National Woman Suffrage Association, *How Women Won It.* (New York: The H.W. Wilson Company, 1940), Appendix 4, pp. 161-164.

		Electoral Vote
1914	MONTANA adopted a constitutional amendment on its first submission.	4
1914	NEVADA adopted a constitutional amendment on its first submission.	3
1917	NORTH DAKOTA secured presidential suffrage by legislative enactment, after defeat of a constitutional amendment in 1914.	5
1917	NEBRASKA secured presidential suffrage by legislative enactment after defeats of a constitutional amendment in 1882 and 1914.	8
1917	RHODE ISLAND secured presidential suffrage by legislative enactment after defeat of a constitutional amendment in 1887.	5
1917	NEW YORK adopted a constitutional amendment after defeat in 1915.	45
1917	ARKANSAS secured primary suffrage by legislative enactment.	9
1918	MICHIGAN adopted a constitutional amendment after defeats in 1874, 1912 and 1913. Secured presidential suffrage by legislative enactment in 1917.	15
1918	TEXAS secured primary suffrage by legislative enactment.	20
1918	SOUTH DAKOTA adopted a constitutional amendment after six prior campaigns for suffrage had been defeated, each time by a mobilization of the alien vote by American-born political manipulators. In that state, as in nine others in 1918, the foreign-born could vote on their "first papers" and citizenship was not a qualification for the vote. The last defeat, in 1916, had been so definitely proved to have been caused by the vote of German-Russians in nine counties that public sentiment, in addition to the war spirit, aroused a desire to make a change in the law which resulted in victory.	5
1918	OKLAHOMA adopted a constitutional amendment after defeat in 1910.	10
1919	INDIANA secured presidential suffrage by legislative enactment in 1917. Rendered doubtful by a court decision the law was re-enacted with but six dissenting votes.	15

		Electoral Vote
1919	MAINE secured presidential suffrage by legislative enactment after defeat of a constitutional amendment in 1917.	6
1919	MISSOURI secured presidential suffrage by legislative enactment after defeat of a constitutional amendment in 1914.	18
1919	IOWA secured presidential suffrage by legislative enactment after defeat of a constitutional amendment in 1916.	13
1919	MINNESOTA secured presidential suffrage by legislative enactment.	12
1919	OHIO secured presidential suffrage by legislative enactment after defeat of referendum on the law in 1917 and of a constitutional amendment in 1912 and 1914.	24
1919	WISCONSIN secured presidential suffrage by legislative enactment after defeat of a constitutional amendment in 1912.	13
1919	TENNESSEE secured presidential suffrage by legislative enactment.	12
1920	KENTUCKY secured presidential suffrage by legislative enactment.	13

Total of presidential electors for whom women were entitled to vote before the 19th Amendment was adopted, 339. (Full number 531)

In 1913 the territory of Alaska had adopted woman suffrage. It was the first bill approved by the Governor.

Part three

Bibliographic Essay

One measure of the success of this book will be the number of its readers who want to learn more about the suffrage movement and the feminism of which it was a part. Two works of reference will be helpful: Albert Kirchmar et al., *The Women's Rights Movement in the United States 1848-1970: A Bibliography and Sourcebook* (Metuchen, N.J.: The Scarecrow Press, 1972) is neither complete nor entirely accurate, but it contains a great deal of important material, including manuscript sources. There are forty-two pages of references on the suffrage movement. The second basic work is *Notable American Women* (Cambridge: Harvard University Press, 1971), 3 vols. In these volumes are found biographies of hundreds of women who were involved in the suffrage movement, including eighty-nine identified as "notable" primarily for their suffrage work. The essays are of high quality and the bibliographical notes are excellent.

Another important group of books are those written or edited by participants in the women's rights movement. The most important is the six volume *History of Woman Suffrage*, edited by Susan B. Anthony, Elizabeth Cady Stanton and Matilda Joslyn Gage, and later by Ida Husted Harper, published between 1881 and 1922. A modern reprint from the Source Book Press is available. Mrs. Stanton's own memoirs, *Eighty Years and More*, appears in various editions, including as a volume in *Elizabeth Cady Stanton as Revealed in Her Letters and Reminiscences*, edited by Theodore Stanton and Harriot Stanton Blatch (New York: Harpers, 1922). Anything Mrs. Stanton wrote is good reading; her lively mind and vigorous personality come through on the printed page. Her coworker Susan B. Anthony had some hand in the authorized biography of herself written by Ida Harper and published in three volumes *The Life and Work of Susan B. Anthony* (Indianapolis: Hollenbeck, 1901). Lucretia Mott appears most vividly in Anna Hallowell, ed., *The Life and Letters of James and Lucretia Mott* (Boston: Houghton Mifflin, 1884), but she is also the subject of a modern biography by Otelia Cromwell, (Cambridge: Harvard University Press, 1958). Lucy Stone, likewise, can be found both in her daughter's biography (Boston: Little, Brown and Co., 1930) and in a more recent one by Elinor Rice Hays, *Morning Star: A Biography of Lucy Stone* (New York: Harcourt-Brace, 1961). Alma Lutz also published biographies of both Stanton and Anthony, *Created Equal* (New York: John Day, 1940) and *Susan B. Anthony* (Boston: Beacon Press, 1959).

Any study of early nineteenth century feminist thought must also include Sarah M. Grimké, *Letters on the Equality of the Sexes and the Condition of Women* (Boston: Issac Knapp, 1838); Angelina Grimké, *Letters to Catherine Beecher* (Boston: Issac Knapp, 1836); and Margaret Fuller, *Woman in the Nineteenth Century* (New York: Greeley and McElrath, 1845).

For later suffragists, Mary Grey Peck, *Carrie Chapman Catt* (New York: H.W. Wilson, 1944) is the work of one of Mrs. Catt's closest friends and a coworker in the suffrage movement. Harriot Stanton Blatch told her story in *Challenging Years* (New York: G.P. Putnam, 1940). Other firsthand accounts of the twentieth-century movement are Caroline Katzenstein, *Lifting the Curtain* (Philadelphia: Dorrance and Co., 1955); Inez Haynes Irwin, *The Story of the Woman's Party* (New York: Harcourt-Brace, 1921); Doris Stevens, *Jailed for Freedom* (New York: Boni and Liveright, 1920, 1921); Carrie Chapman Catt and Nettie R. Schuler, *Woman Suffrage and Politics* (New York: Charles Scribner's Sons, 1926), revised edition. *Victory: How Women Won It*, published by H.W. Wilson in New York in 1940 for the National American Woman Suffrage Association contains eleven lively essays written by participants in the suffrage campaign.

One of the most interesting works by a participant-observer is Helen L. Sumner, *Equal Suffrage* (New York: Harpers, 1901). Sumner was commissioned by the College Equal Suffrage League to make a careful study of the political and social consequences of equal suffrage in the state of Colorado. She proceeded to do this, using statistical analysis and perceptive observation. Mildred Adams, *The Right to be People* (Philadelphia: Lippincott, 1966), though published many years later is the work of a woman who knew the suffragists and took part in the movement in her youth.

For the nineteenth-century suffrage movement there is a bias in the record since the *History of Woman Suffrage* was compiled by the leaders of the National Woman Suffrage Association, and devotes only one chapter to the American Woman Suffrage Association. For the history of the latter, which extends beyond Hays, *Lucy Stone* and Lois Merk, "Massachusetts and the Woman Suffrage Movement," dissertation at Northeastern University in 1961, it is necessary to go to the files of the *Woman's Journal* which will soon be available on microfilm.

For the twentieth-century movement there is bias in all the firsthand accounts insofar as neither wing gives proper credit to the other. Thus Irwin and Stephens write as if NAWSA did not exist, while Maud Wood Park, *Front Door Lobby* (Boston: Beacon Press, 1960) has only harsh things to say about the influence of the Congressional Union and the Woman's Party. Loretta Zimmerman's "Alice Paul and the National Woman's Party," dissertation, Tulane University, 1964 is the work of a careful scholar, but she, too, is a prisoner of her sources and underestimates the work of NAWSA.

Of the secondary materials available, far and away the best is Eleanor Flexner, *Century of Struggle* (Cambridge: Harvard University Press, 1958) to which this essay owes a great deal. Ms. Flexner is presently preparing a revised edition of what has become a classic. Other books deal more or less effectively with particular aspects of the movement. Aileen Kraditor, *Ideas of the Woman Suffrage Movement* (New York: Columbia University Press, 1965) is based on impressive research but reaches sometimes questionable conclusions. Alan Grimes in the *Puritan Ethic and Woman Suffrage* (New York: Oxford, 1967) interprets the suffrage movement as an effort to conserve white Anglo-Saxon "Puritan" values. T.A. Larsen, "Emancipating the West's Dolls, Vassals and Hopeless Drudges," in Roger Daniels, ed., *Essays in Western History in Honor of T.A. Larsen* (Laramie: University of Wyoming Press, October 1971) is a better analysis of the western suffrage movement and should be widely known. Sharon Hartman Strom's forthcoming essay, "Leadership and Tactics in the American Suffrage Movement: A New Perspective From Massachusetts," to be published in the *Journal of American History*, is excellent on the new styles of campaigning.

Ross Evans Paulson, *Women's Suffrage and Prohibition* (Glenview: Illinois: Scott-Foresman, 1973) provides a comparative analysis and is full of suggestive ideas. Josephine Kamm, *Rapiers and Battleaxes* (London: George Allen & Unwin, 1966) is an interesting and straightforward narrative history of the English suffrage movement, with a good chapter on the militants. David Morgan, *Suffragists and Democrats* (East Lansing: Michigan State University Press, 1972) is an English political scientist's effort to explain the final phase of the suffrage movement. The first six chapters cover familiar ground, but the final four chapters put together material not found elsewhere. William O'Neill, *Everyone Was Brave: The Rise and Fall of Feminism in America* (Chicago: Quadrangle, 1970) offers a view of feminism and suffrage sharply at variance with the one found here.

The material in J. Stanley Lemons, *The Woman Citizen* (Urbana: University of Illinois Press, 1973) on the other hand, sustains our interpretation of what happened after the amendment was passed, and effectively disputes O'Neill's thesis.

An adequate bibliography on feminism would be very extensive. Two recent collections of documents provide a good beginning: Alice Rossi, *The Feminist Papers* (New York: Columbia University Press, 1973) and Nancy L.

Cott, *The Root of Bitterness* (New York: E.P. Dutton, 1972). A bibliographical essay in Richard L. Watson and William Cartwright, *The Reinterpretation of American History and Culture* (Washington: The National Council of Social Studies, 1973) will provide the student with a guide to further study.